BENEFACTION OR BONDAGE?

Social Policy and the Aged

M. Leigh Rooke
Former Professor of Gerontology
Medical College of Virginia
Virginia Commonwealth University

C. Ray Wingrove
Professor of Sociology
Department of Sociology and Anthropology
University of Richmond

Library of Congress Catalog Card Number: 79-5437

To the memory of

our mothers

whose love, faith and inner strength

are a gentle heritage of constancy and courage

PREFACE

Having lived intimately from early childhood with
proud and loving family members and friends who were
old, it is not strange that we have viewed old age as a
time of life as valuable as any other. The special considerations accorded family elders were learned very
young, and, in so doing, we learned respect not only for
them but for ourselves as well. Much later, we met
society's ambivalence toward the aged, developed interest in the process of aging, and became keen observers
of the mounting denigration of .old age by the national
cult of youth worshipers.

Increasingly, we grew cognizant of the locked doors,
with the young inside and the old shut out of the social
mainstream. Our studies, especially in sociology, history and psychology, documented the problem and its pervasive, destructive effects. Over 20 years ago, we became members of that small group laboring in the gerontology vineyards, regarded by colleagues as being somewhat strange and by universities as wasting time on an
unimportant and unproductive subject.

Federal monies and programs changed all this, and
the new attention to the aged and to aging seemed to be
a breakthrough long awaited. All now would be improved
and the old would live with dignity, respect and a fair
share in the Nation's plenty. We, too, sought and gained grant monies, and with them a place in the academic
sun. It was not until approximately a decade later that
our frustrations had mounted to a level where evaluation
of the state of the aged could no. longer be avoided, and
questions could no longer be pushed aside. Billions of
dollars had been spent; many thousands of people had become involved. Yet, the question remained, what actually
had been achieved?

Many months of searching out information, analyzing
data and compiling the results have produced disquieting
evidence that the more things change, the more they stay
the same. The billions of dollars spent have not open-
ed doors to full lives for older people, but only to an
anteroom leading nowhere.

Academia's frenzied pursuit of tax dollars reflects
little change in their viewpoint about the aged, only an
enhanced devotion to grantsmanship. The thousands of
advocates for the aged have built hundreds of small - and
not so small - empires devoted to their own perpetuation.
And, the elderly? They have all of the same problems,
for they are at the bottom of the benefit scale and still
segregated out of the mainstream.

Here we have brought together a sampling of the findings from our study, including the nature of change, degree of progress and extent of benefit that have occurred.
We have found our conclusions frightening not only for the
elderly but also for the society of which they are a part.
Our only hope is that some will read the report with perceptive understanding, will evaluate critically the mag-
nitude of the chaos prevailing, and will heed the need
for courageous leadership to right the wrongs of a problem drowning in its solution. Time is critical; the old
do not have time to wait.

Acknowledgements

A warm and heartfelt appreciation is given to the
many who assisted in this search for information and to
the authors of published data which were used so exten-
sively. Our indebtedness also is acknowledged to those
no longer consciously identified, but who have contributed
through the years to our knowledge and understanding, to
our individual growth and development, and to a certain
tenacity in seeking out specific facts when generalizations suggest that truth has been obscured.

A major contribution has been the labor of love by
two readers. First, Betty Booker, a journalist, reviewed
the draft copy for clarity of content and necessary edit-
ing; and second, Joan Girone, a public official, appraised
the potential value of such information to elected and
appointed officials responsible for effective and

efficient community programs and services.

A special thank you must be included to the University of Richmond for financial assistance in preparing the manuscript for publication. And, a special debt of gratitude is acknowledged to James W. Jackson, Reference Librarian, University of Richmond, for obtaining transcripts of reports and other information not easily available.

Another major contribution was made by Louis S. Barretta, Director, Capital Area Agency on Aging for the Richmond, Virginia, Metropolitan Area, who provided copies of updated Federal regulations, policies and guidelines and pertinent statistical reports whenever requested. His gracious assistance did much to facilitate the compilation of necessary data.

To the many elderly men and women who have shared their problems and their proposed reasoned solutions to them, we say a grateful "thank you". They have shown remarkable insight in identifying the trouble, as well as a great deal of apprehension about the potential results of their assigned incompetence. These responsible, practical mature adults are quite aware of what is happening, and they are concerned.

Last, and by no means least, is the affectionate appreciation given to the typist, Miriam M. Rowe. She has contributed not only her skills in producing a final manuscript against numerous obstacles, but she also has tracked elusive references, caught unclear sentences, made practical suggestions and, in myriad ways, demonstrated the interest of a true friend. To her, we gladly acknowledge our indebtedness.

Although extensive use has been made of the work of others and of reports, statistical data and a variety of other information sources, we assume full responsibility for our analysis of data, for interpretation of findings, and for conclusions reached.

M. Leigh Rooke

C. Ray Wingrove

September, 1979

vii

CONTENTS

CENTURIES OF SUSTAINED AMBIVALENCE TOWARD OLD AGE

Chronological age has little meaning except as one aspect of self identity and the establishment of an individual's place in time. For this reason, any chronological designation, such as age 65, for the identification of characteristics or role is at best a convenience label without intrinsic meaning either in the life of an individual or for a social group.

In every society throughout history there has been a certain proportion of old people. This means there are members of the social group who are older than the greater majority of the people in that society. The actual number of these elderly persons could be very small, while the interpretation of "old" itself has been a variable throughout recorded history. A chronological definition of old age is relatively recent in the historical sense, although there is a long tradition of "old" meaning functional age rather than the number of years lived.

Along with an illusive and varying definition of what constitutes old age in humans, there also has been no aspect of life, no phase in the life cycle, as misunderstood as is old age. The very nature of this lack of clarity has fostered a climate for misconceptions and stereotyping, and for generalizing and over simplifying the condition of old age. Evidence of this is found throughout the English language, for it is filled with aphoristic absurdities, such as: "You can't teach an

old dog new tricks," "Once a man and twice a child,"
"The golden years," "Old and wise." These adages
demonstrate well one common belief, that the elderly
are a homogeneous group, that in old age people become
alike. In societies in which old age has a functional
change connotation, this becoming alike occurs at
variable points for individual members on the basis of
skills, abilities and activities. With the modern
designation of age 65 as a finite point at which men and
women become old, the stereotype has become increasingly
hazardous. As average life expectancy has continued to
increase and the point of demarcation for entering old
age has become more rigid, the result is that twentieth
century man spends more and more of his life being old
with all of the constraints placed upon him as elderly.

To be able to anticipate growing old chronologically
as a natural condition of life is a relatively new development for mankind, a phenomenon which can be included
among other twentieth century social innovations. While
it is true that throughout recorded history every society
has had old members, the chronologically very old have
been exceptionally few, with functional old age and
death frequently as early as the second or third decade
of life. Prevalence of average persons living the
Biblical "three score years and ten" was rare indeed
until it became a very recent occurrence.

The social role of the elderly has varied widely
from one historical period to another, and in different
cultures and social groups within a single time period.
One illustration of a favorable view toward being old
can be found in the social order created under Confucian
values in ancient China. There old age was something to
be desired because it brought accompanying status with
added benefits and privileges. Perhaps no culture better
demonstrates the exalted role of elders than does the
ancient Hebrew society, in which patriarchial rule was
absolute in government, in family and in religion. Here
the gray beard was a badge of knowledge, experience, wisdom and authority. In contrast, old age was regarded as
a dismal and worthless condition, a catastrophic misfortune, according to documented records of early Egypt.
Also in the pre-Christian literature of Greece there is
much evidence of a youth cult and depreciation, ridicule
and neglect of the old. The Greek gods were young, strong,
wise and powerful.

If one studies attitudes toward aging and toward
those grown old in a cultural and social historical per-

spective, the attitudinal pattern for the Western world
appears to offer substantial consistency in a progression of positive change. Moving from primitive to
agrarian societies and then to industrial societies,
the dimunition of harshness is apparent. In the early
nomadic life of hunters and food gatherers, basic
necessities were eked out by physical strength and en-
durance, for those who would eat must contribute. With
only rudimentary tools, customs or religions, there was
little cross-generational dependency. Allowing the weak
to perish or even imposing suicide expectations actually
was not without a kind of primitive humanity, since to
live was to suffer and to starve as well as to threaten
survival of the entire tribe. Later, when social groups
settled into community living, engaged in farming and
herding, stored food and shared benefits, the aged and
infirm became a lessened hazard to the group. Additionally, improved tools and utensils were produced; weaving
and crop culture evolved; religious rites were practiced;
and elementary community governances developed. The
elders then became the counselors and teachers. Their
wisdom and experience evoked respect, status, and warm
regard as they continued to contribute to the social
order in less arduous physical roles. It may be that
an agrarian society of family farms and small villages
still offers a more favorable environment for intergenerational roles and respect emanating from a recipro-
cal relationship of mutual advantage. (Simmons, 1945;
Smith, 1950)

Industrialization, on the other hand, further weak-
ened the apparently fragile stability of the aged in
their society. Despite the teachings of the Church, the
emergence of provisions for paupers as a government
responsibility (Elizabethan Poor Laws, 1603), and the
family as a more stable unit of care and protection,
there also was the Puritan work ethic which prescribed
that "if one would eat, he must work." Although wealthy,
landed elderly men exercised limited power, they had
security within their own domains, while in the middle
class there was strong family intergenerational support.
In contrast, among the already downtrodden lower class,
the old were burdens, often neglected, mistreated and
abandoned as non-contributors in the constant quest for
survival.

Yet, in each time period and each stage of social
development there have been pockets of deviation. In
the midst of so much early harshness toward the elderly,
there were some primitive tribes among whom total accept-

3

ance of the aged prevailed and they were cared for, respected, admired and even idolized. In like manner,
there are later evidences of family ties so strong that
meager possessions were shared willingly with elderly
members. (Simmons, 1945; Smith, 1950; Beauvoir, 1970,
et al)

Perhaps the most consistent characteristic found in
historical review of attitudes towards old age is ambivalence. Even when old age is regarded as synonymous
with wisdom and the pinnacle of social status, there are
few instances when negative values for being old do not
occur. Illustrative of this centuries-old ambivalence
are parallel patterns of role and treatment of the aged
that have coexisted through time and diverse cultures.
Such simultaneous and opposing attitudes evolved in the
Orient, in Eastern Mediterranean countries and later
migrated to Western Europe and across the oceans. In
early patriarchial societies in which the elders had
great authority and respect, there also was concomitant
view by the young that old age was unattractive and a
condition not to be desired. And, along with the authority of and respect for mature wisdom, there still was a
constancy of generational conflicts that was expressed
in ridicule and depreciation of the aged by the young.
This latter condition of devaluing and scorning the aged
became exacerbated whenever control by the elders was
diminished. For example, in that period of the Roman
Empire when gerontocracy waned, powers once held by the
old passed to younger hands. Literature from that era
documents well the antagonism, distaste for and contempt
of the young for the old. This pattern is repeated with
varying intensity throughout history.

It has been generally accepted that Christian influences marked a beginning of more consistant humanitarian treatment and care of the old. To the extent
that religious and secular charitable organizations began to provide care and governments instituted some
protective provisions, this is true. At the same time,
however, public attitudes did not parallel Judaeo-Christian precepts. Even simple kindness to elderly persons
has not spread as a coextension of the expansion of
Christianity.

It is interesting to see the effects of the Ren-
aissance rediscovery of humanism insofar as the elderly
are concerned. In art, such creations as frescos and
icons show the old as prophets and scholars, while at
the same time, the stooped, frail and emaciated Father

4

Time also is the picture of an old man. No doubt the
growing Christian emphasis upon charity and the giving
of alms benefitted old people, but it needs to be remembered that even here the emphasis was upon souls to
be saved and not kindness as an end in itself. Along
with the growth of Christian asylums and hospitals,
there continued to be ridicule, mockery and a general
inhumanity to the aged. The old still were few since
average life expectancy was around the mid-twenties
with as many as half of the children dying before their
first birthday. Even among the British male peerage,
for whom more records have been available than for the
lower social classes, estimates of life expectancy have
been in the early thirties for those who survived childhood. (Rosenthal, 1973)

   Another influence affecting the value scale assigned to the old is that attitudes toward old age seem to
have a much stronger historical identification with
attitudes toward illness, deformity and disease than do
other stages of life. This symbolic relationship has
twentieth century strength in the prevalence of the
belief that "old and sick" are synonymous. Since being
"well and strong" has status and "sick and weak" is
undesirable, the "sick, weak and old" label has implicit
in it the connotation of a lesser value, thereby reduc-
ing the old to a limited worth. The fact that this
meaning to old age is now expressed with pity and with
a strong emphasis upon kind and humane treatment only
serves to obscure feeling among the young that the
elderly are burdens to be endured by those of superior
strength, ability and value.

   An historical perspective for attitudes toward aging
and toward persons grown old not only explains modern
stereotypes of old age, but also demonstrates that the
beliefs and attitudes held by members of any generation
are not actually that generation's own. Instead, attitudes are part of one's heritage, altered only slightly
from generation to generation by evolutionary processes
of change. For this reason, twentieth century verbal-
ized intellectual concerns about the growing numbers of
old persons reflect a learned Judaeo-Christian ethic of
equal individual human worth. At the same time emotionally conditioned behavior, even legislated behavior,
continues to reflect the much older cultural heritage of
viewing the old as inept, ineffectual and dependent.
Knowledge of this heritage, with all of its cross cur-
rents and diverse influences, is the beginning of the

development of perceptive understanding, which must be the forerunner of any real attitudinal change.

It now has become particularly important to bring true attitudes about old age honestly into conscious awareness, and to recognize their durability over centuries of transmission from one generation to the next and across oceans and seas. Not only has "old" been institutionalized on the chronological basis of age 65 in the United States, but life expectancy in industrially and technologically developed countries now is established at well over 70 years from birth, the exact projections depending upon nationality, race and sex. (Population Reference Bureau, Inc., 1977.) Not only are vastly larger percentages of these populations growing old, but the old in these societies are growing older. Centenarians are no longer rare, and their number increases. Those past 65 who elude the constraints of restrictive social policy and continue in their customary life styles can be found in positions of power and influence in government and religious organizations, in business, industry and commerce, in banking and education, and in virtually all of the professions. Functional old age and chronologically assigned old age have now reached a collision course that demands permutation of role values if unhappy consequences are to be avoided.

In order to prevent further erosion of roles and values of those no longer young, and to discard the societal burden imposed by the nurture of attitudes centuries old, it now has become necessary to face honestly the remarkable durability of unsupported negative attitudes toward the aged. Terms have changed, but the attitudinal intent remains. From early disposition by killing to advocacy of euthanasia; from almshouses and asylums to the segregated isolation of nursing homes and mental hospitals; from ridicule, abandonment and mistreatment to victimization, denial and benign neglect; from public charity for paupers to government benefits for the poor — the circle of attitudes remains unbroken. Only the language has changed. The "burden" of care the young now bear is, in truth, still the yoke borne so heavily by the old.

Since the place of the aged in the social order has made so little real progress throughout the annals of time, the question must be asked, "Why?" Is it possible that the progression of social and economic change and of scientific discovery has been so imperfect that civilizations remain incapable of evolving social systems in

6

which the builders and creators of one generation can make a contribution to the next, and also be valued for their gifts already given?

REFERENCES

Beauvoir, Simone de. The Coming of Age. G. T. Putnam's
    Sons. New York, New York. 1972. (Published in
    France.)

_____. Old Age. George Weidenfield and
    Nicolson, Ltd. London, England. 1972.

Burgess, E. W. (Editor) Aging in Western Societies.
    University of Chicago Press. Chicago, Illinois.
    1960.

Clark, Margaret and Barbara G. Anderson. Culture and
    Aging. Charles C. Thomas. Springfield, Illinois.
    1967.

Fischer, David Hackett. Growing Old in America. Oxford
    University Press. New York, New York. 1978.

Garrison, Fielding H. An Introduction to the History
    of Medicine. (Revised) Saunders Publishing
    Company. Philadelphia, Pennsylvania. 1929.

Haynes, Maria S. "The Supposedly Golden Age for the Aged
    in Ancient Rome." The Gerontologist, III, No. 1.
    March, 1963.

Isaacs, Bernard, et al. The Survival of the Unfittest.
    Blackwell Scientific Publications. Oxford,
    England. 1971.

Koller, Marvin R. Social Gerontology. Random House.
    New York, New York. 1968.

Palmore, Erdman. The Honorable Elders. Duke Univer-
    sity Press. Durham, North Carolina. 1975.

Population Reference Bureau, Inc. 1977 World Popula-
    tion Data Sheet. Washington, D. C. March, 1977.

_____. Population
    Bulletin: The Elderly in America. Vol. 30, No. 3.
    Washington, D. C. 1975.

Rosenthal, J. T. "Mediaevel Longevity and the Secular
    Peerage, 1350-1500." Population Studies: XXVII,
    2, 1973. London School of Economics. London,
    England.

Rosow, Irving. "Old Age: One Moral Dilemma of an
    Affluent Society." The Gerontologist, 2:1. 1962.

Russell, J. C. British Medieval Population. University
    of New Mexico Press. Albuquerque, New Mexico.
    1948.

Simmons, Leo W. "Aging in Pre-Industrial Societies."
    Handbook of Social Gerontology. Clark Tibbitts,
    Editor. University of Chicago Press. Chicago,
    Illinois. 1960.

_____. The Role of the Aged in Primitive Society.
    Yale University Press. New Haven, Connecticut. 1945.

Smith, T. L. "The Aged in Rural Society." The Aged and
    Society. M. Derber, Editor. Industrial Relations
    Research Associates. Champaign, Illinois. 1950.

Tibbitts, Clark. "Can We Invalidate Negative Stereo-
    types of Aging?" The Gerontologist, 19, No. 1.
    1979.

_____, (Editor) Handbook of Social Gerontol-
    ogy. University of Chicago Press. Chicago,
    Illinois. 1960.

II

A DEMOGRAPHY OF CHANGE AND CONTINUITY
IN THE UNITED STATES

Increasingly, the persistent question is, "Who are the aged?" Is old age identified by functional changes that occur at different times for different individuals, or is it a specific chronological line of demarcation for all humans on the same birth date? This seems to be the point at issue. Neither an examination of the literature nor a survey of public policy reveals either consensus or consistency in definition. Because of these pervasive discrepancies, great caution must be exercised to identify the subject population for any report on characteristics of the old. Failure to do so makes generalizations questionable and any conclusions suspect.

Even public policy in the United States pertaining to older citizens is based on quicksands of vacilation rather than on a bedrock of conviction. For example, chronological age 65 was institutionalized in the United States in 1935, marking the beginning of old age based on automatic eligibility for Social Security old age benefits. In 1956, however, the Social Security Administration arbitrarily selected age 62 for optional eligibility for women to receive reduced benefits. Five years later this alternative "old age" was extended to men. Still another adjustment was made to the Social Security Act when the Older Americans Comprehensive Services Amendment of 1973 became law. At that time, old age benefits became available at 60 years of age.[1]

11

This confusion does not stop with the Social Security Administration. The Federal Administration on Aging, organized as the national advocacy agency for citizens and promulgator of their rights to continue in the mainstream of society, has mandated that its benefactions be bestowed beginning at age 60. These provisions for 60 year olds swelled the numbers of "old" in the nation and reinforced the need for the aging agency services.

Yet another approach to identifying the old can be found in the Department of Labor's designation of the older worker as someone who is more difficult to place because of age. Here the "old" label is applied to workers over 45 years of age. In short, under government sponsorship, the old grow constantly younger. When this is compared with the steadily increasing life expectancy, it is clearly forseeable that one may spend half of his life under the label of "old."

Inasmuch as this situation confuses and obscures actual conditions with regard to the elderly, it seems advisable to delve briefly into characteristics of this population in order to look more objectively at their present status, attitudes and views. This is done with clear knowledge of the wide differences among the "old" labels, as well as of the dangers inherent in accepting any arbitrary chronological cut-off point for being old. Nonetheless, data here reported adhere to the age 65 mark of identification. This is done without even tacit support of the view that age 65 is a valid criterion for being old. The use of this pillar point is merely one of expediency since more statistical data are available and accessible for this age designation, and these data have been maintained for a longer time.

Growth of the Elderly Population of the United States

The aged made up only 4 per cent of the total population in 1900, but they have been increasing in numbers at a much faster rate than has the general population. While the total population nearly tripled from 76 million in 1900 to 215 million in 1975, those 65 and over increased seven-fold, or from 3 million in 1900 to 22+ million in 1975. Today there are approximately 23.5 million people in the U. S. who are 65 or over and this represents approximately 11 per cent of the total population. Furthermore, the U. S. can anticipate a continuing growth in the number and proportion of aged in the total population for many years to come.[2]

Table I

Per Cent of Population 65 and Over by Year, 1900-2020

Year	Number Over 65	Per Cent of Total Pop.
1900	3,000,000	4.1
1960	16,000,000	9.0
1965	18,000,000	9.4
1970	20,050,000	9.9
1975	22,000,000+	11.0+
1980	24,000,000	
1990	27,700,000	
2000	28,800,000	
2010	30,900,000	
2020	40,200,000	13-15

Source: "The Elderly in America," Population Bulletin, Vol. 30, No. 3, 1975. (Population Reference Bureau, Inc., Washington, D. C.) pp. 4-5., and Statistical Notes, National Clearinghouse on Aging, No. 2, August, 1978. Administration on Aging, Office of Human Development Services, U. S. Department of Health, Education and Welfare. Washington, D. C.

It is noted from Table 1 that the rate of growth will slow noticeably between 1990 and 2010 (reflecting the low birth rates during the Depression and up to World War II), but will jump considerably after 2010 due to the coming of age during that decade of the post World War II baby boom babies. Projections should be quite accurate until the year 2020, since these members of the future's elderly are already born.

Another interesting phenomenon occurring among the aging population is that the fastest growing segment is the 75-year-and-over category. In 1900, only 29 per cent of the aged were 75 or older, whereas it is projected that 39 per cent will be in that age bracket by the year 1990.[3] Further it is projected that by the year 1990 those who are 85 years and older will have increased to 9 per cent of the total aged population. Projections to the year 2035 indicate that 18.3 per cent of the total population will be 65 years or over and that almost half of that age group will be 75 or over. In fact, by 2035,

13

one in every 10 aged will be 85 or over.[4]

Table 2

Per Cent of Aged Population 64-75 and 75 and Over by Year

Year

Age	1900	1930	1960	1970	1990
64-74	71	71	66.2	61.9	61.0
75+	29	29	33.8	38.2	39.0

Source: "The Elderly in America," Population Bulletin, Vol. 30, No. 3, 1975. (Population Reference Bureau, Inc., Washington, D. C.) Table 5, p. 11.

Several forces are responsible for the increasing proportion and number of aged in the United States. One of the most important influences is the high fertility rate during the late nineteenth and early twentieth centuries followed, except for the brief period of the post World War II baby boom, by a long and precipitous decline in birth rates. Additionally, the millions of young immigrants to the United States during the first quarter of this century have contributed numerous survivors to the ranks of today's aged. Finally, of course, there has been a tremendous increase in life expectancy since 1900.[5]

Life Expectancy

The average person born in 1900 would expect to live about 47 years as opposed to the 72.4 years of the average person born in 1975.[6] In a more recent report by the Bureau of Census, life expectancy for males born in 1977 is estimated to be 71.8 years and for females, 81.0 years. Contrary to what many believe, this great extension in life expectancy has occurred due to the conquering of childhood and communicable diseases rather than to any medical breakthroughs affecting the later years of life. In other words, an extraordinary drop in infant mortality has allowed more people to live to be old. Actually, those who survive to their 65th birthdays today do not have many more years of life

14

expectancy than did their counterparts of 1900. A person reaching his 65th birthday in 1900 could expect approximately 12 more years of life, while a person reaching that age in 1975 could contemplate fewer than 16 more years, a difference of only about four years.[7]

It is true that life expectancies vary greatly in relation to a number of factors, including sex and race. Women can expect to live longer than men, and whites longer than blacks. Fowles reports that, based on 1975 mortality rates, white females can expect to live about eight years longer than white males, or 77 years versus 69 years. Black females have a life expectancy five years less than white females, but 10 years more than black males.[8] Even though both men and women are living longer, the differential by sex continues to widen, and the trend continues at all ages for both blacks and whites. (See Table 3.) Somewhat at odds with the black-white trend of marked consistency in increasing life expectancy, it is appropriate to note that this is not equally true for all ethnic groups in the United States. For example, the American Indian life expectancy in 1900 was 45 years, and in 1977 had increased to 47 years.

The gaps in life expectancy by race remain except for the very old. At age 75, blacks have a greater life expectancy than do their white counterparts. Table 4 more clearly illustrates how these gaps narrow and/or reverse as cohorts move into the seventh and eighth decades.

Racial and Ethnic Composition

Although there is a higher fertility rate among blacks, there is also a shorter life expectancy. This combined with the fact that most imigrants prior to World War I were white has resulted in a black popu-lation with a much smaller percentage of persons who are 65 and over. In 1975, only 7.4 per cent of the black population was elderly compared with 11.0 per cent of the white. The aged comprise an even smaller percentage of the population of Spanish origin. For reasons shared by blacks, namely, high birthrate and lower life expectancy, only 3.6 per cent of the popu-lation of Spanish origin was 65 years of age or over in 1975.[9]

These facts assume added importance because of the relatively higher visibility of the two groups with

Table 3

Life Expectancy for Various Ages by Race and Sex, 1900-1974

Total	Year 1900-02	1930-31	1955	1965	1974
0 Years	49.2	58.3	69.5	70.2	71.9
65	11.9	12.3	14.2	14.6	15.6
75	7.1	7.3	8.7	9.0	9.8
White Males					
0 Years	48.2	59.1	67.6	67.6	68.9
65	11.5	11.8	13.0	12.9	13.4
75	6.8	7.0	7.9	8.0	8.3
White Females					
0 Years	51.1	62.7	73.6	74.7	76.6
65	12.2	12.8	15.5	16.3	17.6
75	7.3	7.6	9.2	9.6	10.7
Black Males					
0 Years	32.5	47.6	61.2	61.1	62.9
65	10.4	10.9	13.2	12.6	13.4
75	6.6	7.0	10.4	9.8	9.6
Black Females					
0 Years	35.0	49.5	65.9	67.4	71.2
65	11.4	12.2	15.5	15.5	16.7
75	7.9	8.6	12.0	11.2	11.8

Source: Jacob S. Siegel, et al., "Demographic Aspects of Aging and the Older Population in the United States," Current Population Reports, Special Studies, Series P-23, No. 59, May, 1976. Table 5-1, p. 26. U. S. Department of Commerce. Washington, D. C.

Table 4

Life Expectancy for Persons Attaining Ages 65 and 75 Years, 1974

Race and Sex	65 Years	Age	75 Years
All Persons	15.6		9.8
White Males	13.4		8.3
White Females	17.6		10.7
Black Males	13.4		9.6
Black Females	16.7		11.8

Source: Siegel, Current Population Reports, Series P-23, No. 59, op. cit., p. 26.

regard to their generally lower economic status in old age. It needs to be remembered, however, that the black elderly actually number fewer than 2 million and the Spanish origin elderly less than 400,000. Although the completeness of census data for these two groups can be questioned, their combined percentage of the total citizens aged 65 and over in the United States is believed to be less than 10 per cent.

Other racial and ethnic groups with even less representation in the total population, e.g., American Indians, Asian Americans, Eskimos, contribute a very small percentage to the total older population. Additionally, there is even greater question as to the accuracy of census reports for these least visible cultural groups.

Sex Ratio

One result of the higher mortality rate for males is an imbalance in the sex ratio which become apparent by young adulthood. Today there are about 144 women for every 100 men in the 65 and over age bracket, with this imbalance becoming more pronounced as cohorts grow older.[10]

17

Age	Number of Females per 100 Males
65-74	130f/100m
75+	171f/100m
85+	200f/100m

It has been projected that by the year 2000 there will be 154 old women for every 100 old men.[11]

The relationship between age and sex ratio for blacks forms a rough parallel to that of whites. Siegel, et al, summarize the situation as follows:

> The age pattern of sex ratios for the black population is very roughly like that for whites, but the decline with age is less regular and less steep. The "starting" level and the sex ratios at the younger ages are lower than for whites, largely because of the lower sex ratio of births; and the sex ratios as recorded at the older ages are higher, possibly because of the narrower gap between male and female mortality rates in the past and the relatively greater coverage of males than females at the ages above 65 in the census.[12]

It seems apparent that the impact of the sex ratio imbalance has broad social and economic effects for the current generation of elderly in view of their earlier life style and role difference. This difference has gained more official attention statistically than it has from the standpoint of actual real life implications, such as needs in the areas of housing, financial planning and community resources.

Widowhood

The increasing imbalance in the sex ratio as cohorts age means not only that there are many more old women than old men, but that our society contains an increasing number of widows. The greater life expectancy of women combined with the tendency for women to marry men older then themselves results in about 13 years of widowhood for the average married female in our society. In 1975, there were 6.5 million elderly (65+) widows residing in United Stated households who constituted one-third of

18

all persons over 65 years and 53 per cent of all elderly women.[13] Because of factors mentioned previously, the proportion of elderly women who are widows increases with age. By age sixty-five, 36 per cent of women are widows, while widowers are relatively uncommon until age seventy-five.[14]

Table 5

Per Cent of Women 65 Years of Age and Over Who are Widows by Age Category and Race

Age	All Races	White	Black
65+ Years	52.5	51.8	60.2
65-74 Years	41.9	40.8	52.6
75+ Years	69.4	68.9	73.9

Source: Fowles, Donald G., "Elderly Widows," Statistical Memo, No. 33, DHEW Publication No. (OHD) 77-20015, July, 1976. p. 2.

In a 1976 report on elderly widows, Fowles writes,

...the conditions of their existence are considerably different from the elderly population in general. Most widows live alone on relatively low incomes. One-fourth rely on cash incomes below the Federal Government's poverty index. Many have given up their homes and moved to smaller apartments, but housing costs consume a large share of their income. Most do not have automobiles and must rely on other sources of transportation.[15]

Unfortunately, the extent of these conditions has not diminished during the intervening years to the present time.

In addition to the elderly widows living in households, there are another one-half million in nursing homes. They constitute one-half of the entire nursing home population and three-fourths of the women in such institutions.[16] In fact, it is the widow segment of the older population in the United States who appear to represent a high percentage of those who live in inappropriate circumstances, e.g., in nursing homes when

19

their health status does not justify this level of
medical care, or in homes for the aged when constant
custodial surveillance would seem to be counterindi-
cated. These also are the ones who, in the main, have
spent their earlier lives as homemakers and have the
most limited financial resources in old age, an economic pattern that can be expected to change for later
generations of elderly women.

Educational Attainment

        Using such measures as high school graduation and
median years of school completed, the educational
attainment of the present aged falls far below that of
adults in general in the United States. In 1975, three-
fifths of the adult population were high school graduates compared with only one-third of the over 65 aged
population. The median school years completed were nine
years for those 65+ but 12.3 years for those ages 25-64.[17]

        This negative correlation between age and educational
attainment reflects a number of factors, such as: 1)
increasing opportunities and expectations for the younger
population, 2) rising socio-economic status of Americans
during the past four decades, and 3) the high proportion
of foreign born among today's aged. Nevertheless, the
gap in level of educational achievement between the old
and the rest of the adult population is rapidly closing.
By 1990, it is estimated that the per cent of high school
graduates 65 years and over will be only about one-third
below the per cent for the entire adult population.[18]

        It should be noted that these statistics reflect
the escalating emphasis during the past 40 years upon
mandatory school attendance and the easy availability
of opportunities for education in institutional settings.
In contrast, the current older generation had less
universally available formal education beyond a basic
elementary foundation. Further, the value standards
which molded their development emphasized acquisition
of practical skills over academic achievement. Many of
today's older citizens have been highly skilled artisans
who learned on the job under skilled and respected
master craftsmen. In short, the elderly are not an
ignorant population, but rather they are less tutored
in formal educational programs commonplace today. These
are the men and women whose skills, knowledge and capability built a nation more productive than any other.

20

Employment

In 1950, fifteen years after Social Security became law, almost 50 per cent of the aged male population was in the labor force, but there has been a steady percentage decline in their employment since then. In 1975, about 22 per cent of the aged population remained in the labor force, representing about 21 per cent of the male, and 10.5 per cent of the female population 65 and over.[19] In contrast with males, however, aged females in the labor force continued to increase through 1970 except for a small decrease in the 70-74 age group. Not until 1975 did the female pattern begin to follow that of males. (See Table 6.)

This decline of the elderly population in the labor force reflects a number of societal changes, including, 1) the increased popularity of voluntary retirement programs, 2) the decline in self-employment, 3) enforcement of mandatory retirement policies, and 4) the decline of such industries as railroads and agriculture which have employed many older workers. Paralleling this decline in employment of older workers, it also needs to be noted that there still are many men and women actively seeking employment in the Nation's labor force. Approximately 5 per cent of the men between 65 and 75 years of age and roughly 6 per cent of women in that age group were reported to be seeking work in 1970. This does not include those over 75 years, among whom were 11 per cent of the women and 5.7 per cent of the men who sought employment.[20] Brotman reports that about 44 per cent of older workers hold part-time jobs compared to 16 per cent of those under 65 years.[21] These findings are consistent with expectations not only because a majority of adults under 65 hold full-time employment, but also because this older generation is one in which need for income could be expected to be solved by work. An additional factor could be that those retired under rigid age determined retirement rules would include some who did not wish to do so and sought other jobs elsewhere.

Income

Income for retired persons is derived from four major sources. Most important and far reaching are incomes from Social Security and pensions. Second in importance as an income resource is wages, with some-

Table 6

Per Cent of Aged in Labor Force by Sex and Age Category
1950, 1960, 1970 and 1975

Per Cent in Labor Force

Age	1950		1960		1970		1975	
	M	F	M	F	M	F	M	F
65-69	59.7	13.0	44.0	16.5	39.3	17.2	33.3	14.3
70-74	38.7	6.4	28.7	9.6	22.5	9.1	{ 14.9	5.2
75+	18.7	2.6	15.6	4.3	12.1	4.7	{	

Source: Population Bulletin, "The Elderly in America," A publication of the Population Reference Bureau, Inc., Vol. 30, No. 3, p. 13, 1975. Washington, D. C.

thing less than one-quarter of elderly couples earning one-half or more of their financial support. The third source in numbers of elderly people affected is assets from investments and savings. Finally and fourth is income from public assistance.[22]

It may come as a surprise to those who have become accustomed to thinking of old and poverty as synonymous to learn that 20 per cent of the families headed by a person 65 or older had annual incomes in excess of $15,000 in 1975. (See Table 7.)

As a matter of fact, the aged have been making rather noticeable financial gains in the last 15 years. The decade of the sixties was one of economic progress for young and old alike. During this decade the median income of families headed by persons 65 and over increased by one-third, and that of persons 65 and over who lived alone climbed 41 per cent. The seventies have not been as generous to the older citizenry, but even here gains have been made. From 1970 to 1976 the median income of young families and individuals (25-64 years of age) grew by only 4 per cent. Yet even during this period of economic decline, the median income of families and individuals 65 years and over increased 18 per cent and 22 per cent respectively.[23] (See Table 8.)

As one might expect, the rise in median income among the aged has been accompanied by a decline in the proportion living below the poverty level since 1970.[24] At the time of the White House Conference on Aging in November, 1971, a major concern was with the one-quarter of the elderly living below the poverty level. In 1975, there were 3.3 million persons 65 years old and over living below the poverty level, or 15.3 per cent of the total aged population.[25] This decline since 1972 has occurred in part as a result of several recent changes in Social Security benefits and regulations. Social Security payments increased by 20 per cent during the last quarter of 1972 and again by 11.1 per cent in 1974. Since 1975, the cost-of-living escalator clause in the Social Security law has been in effect. The total increase in Social Security benefits between 1965 and 1975 totals approximately 75 per cent, and, due to inflation, continues to rise.[26] Also beginning in 1972, widows received the entire amount of the benefits of their deceased spouses instead of the former 82.5 per cent,[27] and Social Security recipients aged 65 and over now can earn $4,500 annually without being penalized, and this will increase each year until it reaches $6,000 in 1982.

Table 7

Per Cent Distribution of Families and Unrelated
Individuals by Income and Age, 1975

Income in 1975	Families		Unrelated Individuals	
	Head 25 to 64	Head 65+	25 to 64	65+
Under $5,000.........	8.7	23.5	35.2	72.6
$5,000 to $9,999.....	17.1	37.7	30.4	20.2
$10,000 to $15,000...	22.6	18.8	20.6	4.5
$15,000 and over.....	51.6	20.0	13.9	2.7

Source: "Income and Poverty Among the Elderly, 1975." Statistical Reports On Older Americans, No. 2. April, 1977. DHEW.

24

Table 8

Median Income in Constant 1975 Dollars[1]/ of Families
and Unrelated Individuals by Age, 1970 to 1975

Year	Families			Unrelated Individuals		
	Head 25-64 years	Head 65+ years		25-64 years	65+ years	
		Amount	As percent of 25-64		Amount	As percent of 25-64
1975	$15,332**	$8,057	52.6	$7,441	$3,311*	44.5
1974 (revised)	15,824	8,191	51.8	7,460	3,257	43.7
1974	15,730**	7,965	50.6**	7,291**	3,226*	44.2*
1973	16,365**	7,783	47.6	7,751**	3,300**	42.6
1972	15,962**	7,678**	48.1	7,336	3,084**	42.0**
1971	15,182	7,247*	47.7*	7,310	2,922**	40.0**
1970	15,151	7,004	46.2	7,321	2,704	36.9
Change, 1970 to 1975.	181**	1,053**	6.4**	120	607**	7.6**

1/ All medians were adjusted for changes in cost of living and are shown in 1975 dollars.
*   Indicates statistically significant change from previous year at the 90-95 per cent
    confidence level (1.6-2.0 standard errors).
** Indicates statistically significant change from previous year at the 95 per cent or
    higher confidence level (2.0 standard errors or more).
NOTE: In computing and testing the difference between 1973 and 1974, unrevised figures were
       used for both years. For the difference between 1974 and 1975, revised figures were
       used for both years.

Source: "Income and Poverty Among the Elderly, 1975." Statistical Reports On Older Americans,
         No. 2. April 1977. DHEW.

25

In spite of these gains, far too many of the aged still live below the poverty or near-poverty level. Defining "near-poverty" as 125 per cent of the poverty threshold, 5.5 million older Americans were living below the near-poverty level in 1975. This burden of poverty is not equally distributed, but falls most heavily upon the non-white population and upon single persons, particularly single women. For example, in 1975, 36.3 per cent of the aged black population fell below the poverty level, as did 31 per cent of all elderly unrelated individuals.[28] This situation is further dramatized by the fact that approximately 30 per cent of all unrelated white females were below the poverty level, compared with almost 69 per cent of black unrelated females so classified.[29]

Elderly persons living alone or in a non-family situation continue to be the group with the greatest economic problems. In 1975, 8 per cent (about 400,000) had incomes under $1,500 a year, and 2.5 million had incomes between $1,500 and $3,000; this was a total of 42 per cent, nearly 3 million persons, with sub-marginal incomes. This contrasts sharply with the 7 per cent of families, less than one-half million, headed by persons 65 years of age or older whose incomes were below $3,000. None of these figures shows the deflated purchasing power of the dollar reflected in the 9 per cent increase in the Consumer Price Index between 1974 and 1975.[30]

Universally applied criteria in identifying the poor can be very misleading. The Federal government currently considers rural-urban differences in assigning the label "poor," but systematically ignores other factors, such as life styles, geographic locations, obligations and responsibilities, health status, etc., all of which can have enormous impact upon the purchasing power of the elderly person's dollar.

Another point for consideration is the reported 1.3 million elderly individuals who live in other persons' households when those households are not classified as "poor." Such old persons also are not counted as "poor." A final discrepancy in available statistics is aged individuals in institutions, including nursing homes. All of these hidden elderly poor could raise the category of "poor" and "near poor" to even higher numbers.[31]

Estimates of the percentage of pre-retirement income needed to maintain the same standard of living in post-retirement vary from 50 to 75 per cent.[32] This, too, is

26

grossly misleading, since for some in the lower income
bracket it well could be that the need is 100 per cent
and still remains less than adequate. All of thes serves
to demonstrate that judgments and policies based on
national averages and formula-based needs identification
may greatly inflate - or deflate - actual needs, leading to rigidities in programming that may be self-defeat-
ing.

When a person retires he automatically eliminates
job expenses, such as, work uniforms or work related
clothing costs, transportation and other employment
associated items. Additionally, he often is able to replace some of the formerly purchased services with his
own labors. Tax expenses will usually be lower, including cessation of Social Security payments and reduced
income taxes, among others. By this time in life,
ordinarily the family dependents upon the income are
fewer; homes are now fully furnished. For nearly 80
per cent of elderly home owners, the houses are mortgage
free, and approximately 67 per cent of the aged own their
homes.[33] For a substantial number of 65-year-old
retirees, there now are lower property tax rates for
homes. And, although the cost of Medicare has continued
to rise at a discouraging rate, it still is considered
to be a cheaper health insurance than individual or
group health care protection for those in the working
years. For those who are medically indigent, Medicaid
is available. Even with these Federal health benefit
programs, however, there are serious problems. Among
these are: 1) the steadily rising cost of Medicare insurance, 2) the limitations in its coverage, and 3) for both
Medicare and Medicaid, the regulatory constraints and
rigidity of procedural controls. But these are national
problems and not merely income related.

Financial circumstances, however, should be bright-
er for future aged than they are for those who are now
old. Tomorrow's elderly will be better educated and
will have worked in higher paying jobs. More women will
have worked and will be eligible for their own benefits,
and more workers in general will qualify for company
pensions in addition to Social Security. And, hopefully,
the elimination of inequities in educational and job
opportunities will reduce the economic disparities among
previously less favored groups in the society.[34]

Geographic Distribution and Internal Migration

     The aged tend to live in large heavily populated
states. Two states, California and New York, now have
more than 2 million aged each, and five states, Pennsylvania, Florida, Texas, Illinois and Ohio, have more
than one million each.[35] Twenty-five per cent of the
entire aged population live in California, New York and
Pennsylvania. The addition of Florida, Texas, Illinois
and Ohio to the list accounts for another 20 per cent,
bringing the total to 45 per cent of the aged in seven
states.[36]

     The states most heavily populated by the elderly,
however, are not necessarily the ones with the largest
percentage of their populations over 65 years of age.
In 1975, although Florida led the states with 16.1 per
cent of its population 65 years and over as the result
of in-migration, and Arkansas ranked second because of
younger out-migration, four Western states, namely,
Iowa, Nebraska, Missouri and Kansas, fell into third,
fourth, fifth and sixth places respectively with an
excess of 12 per cent of their populations elderly.
As in the case of Arkansas, the Western states cited
represented home-grown elderly whose percentages have
swelled as the old remain on the farms and in the
villages, while the young seek their fortunes in cities
outside the region.[37] In short, older citizens are a
relatively stable population. Their migration rates
are low. But, when they do move, they are likely to head
for retirement communities in the Sun Belt, such as
Florida or Arizona, or to small towns. Those living in
the rural hinterlands and the central cities are the least
likely to move.

     If the farm population and urban fringe are excluded,
the larger the place, the lower the percentage of elderly
people. The highest proportion of the aged is found in
small towns followed by urban areas of 2500 to 10,000,
followed by urban communities of 10,000 to 50,000, and
finally by the rural farm and urban fringe. Those living
in large urban communities are more heavily represented
in the central city.[38] These facts concerning distribution and clustering of the elderly are totally relevant
to social planning based upon understanding. This is a
matter not to be simplistically treated by formula-based
Federal funds distribution, but has far more complex ramifications. In no segment of the population is there
greater diversity of life styles, perceived needs or

value orientations than among older people. Only those
bred in the traditions and cultures of these differences
will be able to comprehend the all important human components of problem solving.

Health

Recognizing that aging does not cause illness or
disease, it is true that elderly persons do have more
chronic ailments (those lasting three months or longer),
such as, arthritis, hypertension, hearing loss, visual
impairment, heart disease, than do younger people. The
proportion of the population experiencing at least one
chronic condition increases from 23 per cent of those
under 17 years of age to 85 per cent for those 65 and
over. In spite of this, fewer than 14 per cent of older
persons report that their chronic conditions prevent
them from carrying out their major activities. In contrast, the aged have fewer acute illnesses than does the
younger population, e.g., 1.1 acute conditions for those
65 and over compared to the 3.6 such conditions for
children under 6 years. When acute illness does occur,
however, the recovery time generally is a bit longer for
the older person.[39]

The Harris Study found that 51 per cent of the
general public under 65 years of age viewed serious
health problems as a primary problem of those over age
65, while they were so viewed by only 21 per cent of the
elderly themselves.[40] This latter evaluation by the
elderly is consistent with the frequently quoted Federal
statistics issued in the early seventies that showed
approximately 81 per cent of persons aged 65 and over
leading independent lives in their communities and
managing their own affairs, about 14 per cent functioning
with limitations that required some assistance from their
families, and only roughly 5 per cent (sometimes reported
as 4 per cent) living in institutions.[41] In the latter
category, the majority were over 75 years of age. These
data coupled with reports of inappropriate placement of
aged persons in institutions, of insufficient health
maintenance available to this group, and of a dearth of
personnel in the health industry adequately qualified to
treat geriatric patients, all combine to raise questions
concerning the relationship between actual health status
of the old and their potential for health. One example
of the validity of such a question is the report that
the occurrence of widowhood among older women frequently
precipitates entering a nursing home or other custodial
care institution as a place of residence.

Family and Living Arrangements

As shown in Table 9, most older people can be found living in private households in the community. A majority of these also live in a family situation.(See Table 10.) It is true that the proportion of men living in families far exceeds that for women, since the latter are more likely to be widowed and alone. This condition is reinforced by the fact that remarriage among men following the death of a spouse is more prevalent than among women, reflecting both the greater availability of unmarried women in their age group and the commonly accepted practice of men marrying younger women. Another aspect of living alone, which shows an increasing trend especially among older women, is that women are more than twice as likely to maintain a household by themselves than are older men, 36 per cent versus 14.2 per cent. These figures pertain although the percentage of elderly living in institutions increases with age, but still accounts for fewer than 5 per cent of all those who are over 65 years of age.

Another aspect of the social living patterns in later life is the reluctance of many older persons to live with their children, although there is evidence that a high percentage of them live in relatively close proximity to one or more children and see them frequently. According to the Harris Survey, 55 per cent of those age 65 and above had seen their children "within the last day or so" and 26 per cent "within the last week or two," while another 8 per cent extended the time lapse to "a month."[43] Studies by Stehouwer (1965), Shanas, et al (1968), Butler and Lewis (1973), and others show comparable evidence of parent-adult child contacts. Even when moving from one geographical area to another, the travel distance between the retirees and one or more children often is reported to be a consideration.

According to U. S. Census Bureau data, a substantial number of elderly persons live in substandard housing, an estimated 30 per cent, with a higher prevalence of housing with major defects among the aged poor, as would be expected. Criteria applied in this determination include not only age, condition and dollar value of the property, but also lack of inside running water (15 per cent), inside flush toilet (30 per cent), bathroom with hot water (40 per cent), central heat (50 per cent).[44] In 1975, a study of the housing of older rural citizens showed 20 per cent lacked "complete plumbing facilities."[45]

30

Table 9

Living Arrangements of the Population 55 Years Old and Over, by Age and Sex, 1965, 1970 and 1975*

Living Arrangements and Year	Male				Female			
	55-64 Yrs.	65-74 Yrs.	75 Yrs. & Over	65 Yrs. & Over	55-64 Yrs.	65-74 Yrs.	75 Yrs. & Over	65 Yrs. & Over
1975								
In households	98.1	97.1	92.6	95.6	98.8	97.5	90.0	94.4
Living alone	7.6	12.1	18.2	14.2	17.4	32.9	40.6	36.0
Spouse present	80.7	79.6	63.3	74.0	66.1	46.2	20.1	35.6
Living with someone else	9.7	5.4	11.2	7.4	15.3	18.4	29.3	22.8
Not in households[1]	1.9	2.9	7.4	4.4	1.2	2.5	10.0	5.6
1970								
In households	97.6	96.4	93.7	95.5	98.4	97.6	91.1	95.0
Living alone	7.2	11.3	19.1	14.1	17.1	31.6	37.0	33.8
Spouse present	82.3	75.2	60.4	69.9	63.8	43.5	19.1	33.9
Living with someone else	8.1	9.9	11.2	11.5	17.5	22.4	35.0	27.4
Not in households[1]	2.4	3.6	6.3	4.5	1.6	2.4	8.9	5.0
1965								
In households	97.5	97.5	93.6	96.2	98.4	97.4	92.0	95.3
Living alone	7.0	11.7	15.7	13.1	15.5	27.9	29.9	28.6
Spouse present	80.3	75.3	54.0	67.9	63.8	43.3	19.0	34.1
Living with someone else	10.2	10.5	23.9	15.2	19.1	26.1	43.1	32.6
Not in households[1]	2.5	2.5	6.4	3.8	1.6	2.6	8.0	4.7

* Excludes Armed Forces on post.   [1] Population in institutions and other group quarters.

Source: Taken from Jacob S. Siegel, et al, "Demographic Aspects of Aging and the Older Population in the United States," Current Population Reports, Special Studies, Series P-23, No. 59, May, 1976. p. 48.

31

Table 10

Family Status of the Population 65 Years Old and Over, by Sex
1965, 1970, and 1975

(Total resident population excluding members of the Armed Forces on post. Figures are for March of year indicated.)

Family Status	1975		1970		1965	
	Male	Female	Male	Female	Male	Female
Percent, total	100.0	100.0	100.0	100.0	100.0	100.0
In families	79.8	56.1	79.2	58.5	80.3	62.9
Head	76.1	8.5	72.9	9.8	71.3	10.7
Wife	(X)	35.0	(X)	33.3	(X)	33.3
Other relative	3.7	12.7	6.3	15.4	9.0	18.9
Primary individual	14.8	37.3	14.9	35.2	13.9	30.6
Secondary individual	1.2	1.2	2.4	1.9	2.3	2.2
Inmate of institution	4.2	5.3	3.6	4.4	3.5	4.3

X Not applicable
Source: Taken from Jacob S. Siegel, et al, "Demographic Aspects of Aging and the Older Population in the United States," Current Population Reports, Special Studies, Series P-23, No. 59, May, 1976. p. 48.

On these bases, needs for Federal housing assistance are promulgated. In contrast, however, the Harris Study reported that only 4 per cent of the elderly surveyed considered poor housing to be a "very serious" problem, in contrast with the 35 per cent of the respondents under age 65 who so regarded it for the elderly. When the category of "somewhat serious" was added in the Survey, the responses are 11 per cent and 35 per cent respectively.[46]

The discrepancy between officially reported housing conditions based upon late twentieth century value standards and the expressed views of older Americans can be explained on the basis of perceived needs and values. Although there is a matter of money and the economic ability to make changes, there is an even stronger factor of psychological conditioning in the differing viewpoints. Some of the old people do not want to change, not even for something better; the familiar is mentally comfortable. Life style is a part of them and the neighborhood bond is strong for both people and things. Further, the inside toilet never known is not now a necessity. Numerous examples of elderly rural residents with adequate incomes can be found where the wood stove is central and the inside bathroom, or even basic plumbing, as well as other modern amenities are lacking; yet they reject change and consider their lives to be good and their homes comfortable. They live as did their fathers before them, and they are emotionally secure. These conditions pertain not only in rural but also in urban communities.[47]

Here, once again, generalization and national programs premised in simplistic cause and effect relationships can be misleading. In order to separate perceived acceptable alternative life styles from the imposed handicaps of unrelieved poverty, it is necessary to probe carefully, to analyze objectively and to plan with those affected in the individual communities of the Nation. This is not a matter to be dealt with summarily by administrative fiat and absentee social planners.

Summary

Thus the picture of the aged in the United States is one of great diversity and heterogeneity, of varying circumstances and conditions. The only true commonality to be found is that they are chronologically older than the rest of the citizens. They are not a stagnant portion of the population in any sense of the word and they are widely different one from another in physical, social, intellectual, economic, cultural characteristics, in life style and in hopes and aspirations.

Not only has their number grown at an accelerated rate in the twentieth century, but this population can be expected to grow rapidly in the foreseeable future, while their characteristics can be expected to change with equal rapidity. A better educated and more economically secure aged population may be less docile, making more demands for continuity of social role and their rights to it than has been done by earlier generations of elderly.

Increasing life expectancies combined with anticipated better health into old age and a continuing trend toward voluntary early retirement can be expected to have two results. One is that there will be more years of healthy retirement with insistence upon continued participation in social actions and decisions. A second repercussion to be anticipated concerns the increasing proportion of the old who are over 75 years of age and, in fact, over 85, who will require a new look at the provisions of health services and the service delivery priorities as they are in force in the health industry today. Preventive health care and maintenance therapies for the elderly, so long ignored, will become not only a humanitarian demand by the old, but also an economic necessity for the young.

The rapidly increasing number of older women relative to older men may have ramifications for the social order yet to be anticipated. Surely the rising numbers of those living alone will necessitate a hard look at the rigid and limited housing choices available to the old who seek on-going independence according to life style preferences and who fear institutionalization.

Even so cursory a review of characteristics and conditions of the over 65 age population in the United States demonstrates quite adequately their wide differences and the unfortunate futility of any attempts to reduce them to mirror likenesses one of the other. Problems do exist; some problems are shared by certain segments of the older population; and some old people have critical needs and deprivations. But, while recognizing these conditions as fact, perhaps none of these problems is so great nor so threatening as is that of conceptualizing the elderly as a like population of the whole. Their diversity is their paramount characteristic.

FOOTNOTES

1
"The Elderly in America," Population Bulletin, Vol. 30,
   No. 3, 1975. Population Reference Bureau, Inc.,
   Washington, D. C. pp. 3-4.

2
Ibid., pp. 4-5. Also see Donald G. Fowles, "Some
   Prospects for the Future Elderly Population,"
   Statistical Reports on Older Americans, No. 3,
   January, 1978. DHEW Publication No. (OHDS) 78-20288.
   Washington, D. C.

3
"The Elderly in America," op. cit., pp. 11-12, and
   Fowles, op. cit., p. 3.

4
Fowles, op. cit., pp. 3 and 5.

5
Ibid., p. 6.

6
Report from U. S. Department of Health, Education and
   Welfare, National Center for Health Statistics.
   (Verbal communication)

7
Jacob S. Siegel, et al. "Dempgraphic Aspects of Aging
   and the Older Population in the United States,"
   Current Population Reports, Special Studies, Series
   P-23, No. 59, May, 1976. pp. 26-27.

8
Fowles, op. cit., p. 6.

9
Siegel, op. cit., p. 15.

10
Ruth B. Weg. The Aged: Who, Where, How Well (Education,
   Health, Income, Marital Status). Paper presented at
   Training Session for College Faculty, Williamsburg,
   Virginia. August 16-19, 1976.

11
Facts About Older Americans 1975. DHEW Publication No.
    (OHD) 75-20006.

12
Siegel, op. cit., p. 15.

13
Donald G. Fowles. "Elderly Widows," Statistical Memo,
    No. 33, DHEW Publication No. (OHD) 77-20015, July,
    1976. p. 1, and James Peterson and Michael P. Briley.
    Widows and Widowhood. Association Press. New York.
    1977.

14
Robert C. Atchley. The Social Forces in Later Life.
    Wadsworth Publishing Company, Belmont, California.
    1977. pp. 186-189.

15
Fowles, "Elderly Widows," op. cit., p. 5.

16
Donald G. Fowles. "Some Prospects for the Future
    Elderly Population," Statistical Reports on Older
    Americans, No. 3. U. S. Department of Health,
    Education and Welfare, Administration on Aging,
    National Clearinghouse on Aging. Washington, D. C.
    January, 1978. p. 7.

17
Siegel, op. cit., p. 49.

18
Ibid.

19
Ibid. pp. 49-51.

20
Employment Status and Work Experience. Subject Report
    PC (2)-6A. U. S. Bureau of the Census. U. S.
    Government Printing Office. Washington, D. C.   1973.
    p. 2.

21
Herman B. Brotman. "Who Are the Aged?" Paper deliver-
    ed at "A Working Conference: What Should We Teach
    About Aging?" New York Association of Gerontolo-
    gical Educators, New York University, November, 1974.
    p. 16.

36

22
"The Elderly in America," op. cit., p. 13.

23
Fowles, "Some Prospects for the Future Elderly Population," op. cit., p. 13.

24
Siegel, op. cit., p. 55.

25
Fowles, "Income and Poverty Among the Elderly," op. cit.,
p. 4.

26
James D. Manney, Jr. Aging in American Society. Insti-
tute of Gerontology, University of Michigan-Wayne
State University. Ann Arbor, Michigan. 1975. p. 124.

27
Fowles, "Income and Poverty Among the Elderly." op.
cit., p. 2, and Time, January 15, 1973. p. 68.

28
Fowles, "Income and Poverty Among the Elderly," op.
cit., p. 7, and Tables 5 and 7.

29
Siegel, op. cit., p. 55.

30
Herman B. Brotman. "Income and Poverty in the Older
Population in 1975," The Gerontologist, Vol. 17,
No. 1, February, 1977. p. 24.

31
Manney, op. cit., p. 124.

32
Robert J. Havighurst. "The Future Aged," Paper presented at the Fourth Annual Seminar in Gerontology,
Madison College, Harrisonburg, Virginia. June 15,
1977.

33
Richard Davis. (Editor) Housing for the Elderly.
University of Southern California, Ethel Percy Andrus
Gerontology Center. Los Angeles, California. 1973.
p. 13.

34
Fowles, "Some Prospects for the Future Elderly Population," op. cit., p. 15.

35
Intercom: The International Newsletter on Population, Vol. 4, No. 3, March, 1976. A Publication of Population Reference Bureau, Inc. Washington, D. C.

36
Siegel, op. cit., p. 16.

37
Ibid., p. 18.

38
Ibid., p. 23.

39
Atchley, op. cit., Chapter 6.

40
The Myth and Reality of Aging in America. Survey conducted by Louis Harris and Associates, Inc. The National Council on the Aging, Inc. Washington, D. C. June, 1976. p. 30.

41
Working With Older People: Vol. III. The Aging Person: Needs and Services. U. S. Department of Health, Education and Welfare, Public Health Service, Rockville, Maryland, 1970. p. 26.

42
Atchley, op. cit., p. 118.

43
The Myth and Reality of Aging in America, op. cit., p. 166.

44
Ira S. Robbins. Housing the Elderly. White House Conference on Aging: Topical Papers. Washington, D. C. 1971.

45
Robert C. Atchley and Sheila J. Miller. "Housing of the Rural Aged," in Environments and the Rural Aged, Robert C. Atchley (Editor). The Gerontological Society. Washington, D. C. 1975.

46
    The Myth and Reality of Aging in America, op. cit.,
    pp. 29-32.

47
    M. Fried. "Grieving for a Lost Home." People and
    Buildings, R. Guttman (Editor). Basic Books.
    New York, New York. 1972. pp. 229-248, and James
    E. Birren. "The Aged in Cities," The Gerontologist,
    Vol. IX, No. 3. Washington, D. C. 1969. pp. 163-
    169.

                          REFERENCES

Atchley, Robert C. (Editor). Environments and the Rural
    Aged. The Gerontological Society. Washington,
    D. C. 1976.

_____. The Social Forces in Later Life.
    Second Edition. Wadsworth Publishing Company, Inc.
    Belmont, California. 1977.

Birren, James E. "The Aged in Cities," The Gerontologist,
    Vol. IX, No. 3. Washington, D. C. 1969.

Brotman, Herman B. "Who are the Aged?" Delivered at "A
    Working Conference: What Should We Teach About Aging?"
    New York State Association of Gerontological Edu-
    cators. New York University. November 14, 1974.

Butler, Robert N. and Myra I. Lewis. Aging and Mental
    Health. The C. V. Mosby Company. St. Louis,
    Missouri. 1973.

Davis, Richard H. (Editor) Housing for the Elderly.
    Ethel Percy Andrus Gerontology Center. University
    of Southern California. Los Angeles, California.
    1973.

"Elderly in America, The." Population Bulletin, Vol. 30,
    No. 3. 1975. Population Reference Bureau, Inc.
    Washington, D. C.

Employment Status and Work Experience. Subject Report PC
    (2)-6A. U. S. Bureau of the Census. U. S. Govern-
    ment Printing Office. Washington, D. C. 1973.

Facts About Older Americans 1975. U. S. Department of
    Health, Education and Welfare. Publication No.
    (OHD) 75-20006. U. S. Government Printing Office,
    Washington, D. C.

Fowles, Donald G. "Some Prospects for the Future
    Elderly Population." Statistical Reports on Older
    Americans. U. S. Department of Health, Education
    and Welfare. Washington, D. C. January, 1978.

_____. "Income and Poverty Among the Elderly:
    1975." Statistical Reports on Older Americans.
    No. 2. U. S. Department of Health, Education and
    Welfare. Washington, D. C. April, 1977.

_____. "Elderly Widows." Statistical Memo
    No. 33. DHEW Publication No. (OHD) 77-20015. U. S.
    Government Printing Office. Washington, D. C.
    July, 1976.

Guttman, R. (Editor) People and Buildings. Basic Books.
    New York, New York. 1972.

Havighurst, Robert J. "The Future of Aging." Paper
    presented at Fourth Annual Seminar in Gerontology.
    Madison College. Harrisonburg, Virginia. June,
    1977.

Hendricks, Jon and C. Davis Hendricks. Aging in Mass
    Society: Myths and Realities. Winthrop Publishers,
    Inc. Cambridge, Massachusetts. 1977.

Intercom: The International Newsletter on Population.
    Vol. 4, No. 3. March, 1976. Population Reference
    Bureau, Inc. Washington, D. C.

Manney, James D., Jr. Aging in American Society.
    Institute of Gerontology. University of Michigan-
    Wayne State University. Ann Arbor, Michigan. 1975.

Myth and Reality of Aging in America, The. Survey con-
    ducted by Lewis Harris and Associates, Inc. The
    National Council on the Aging, Inc. Washington,
    D. C. 1976.

Noll, Paul F. "Housing: An Alphabet Soup of Agencies Fails."
    Perspective on Aging. Vol. VII, No. 1. January/
    February, 1978.

Palmore, Erdman. The Honorable Elders. Duke University Press. Durham, North Carolina. 1975.

Robbins, Ira S. Housing the Elderly. White House Conference on Aging. Washington, D. C. 1971.

Shanas, Ethel and Gordon F. Streib. (Editors) Social Structure and the Family. Prentice-Hall, Inc. Englewood Cliffs, New Jersey. 1965.

Siegel, Jacob S., et al. "Demographic Aspects of Aging and the Older Population in the United States." Current Population Reports, Special Studies, Series P-23, No. 59. U. S. Department of Commerce. Washington, D. C. May, 1976.

Social Security Programs Throughout the World, 1977. U. S. Department of Health, Education and Welfare. Social Security Administration Office of Records and Statistics. Research Report, No. 50. Washington, D. C.   .

Statistical Memo, No. 31. DHEW Publication No. (OHD) 75-20013. U. S. Government Printing Office. Washington, D. C. May, 1975.

Statistical Notes. From the National Clearinghouse on Aging. No. 1. DHEW Publication No. (OHDS) 78-20040. U. S. Government Printing Office. Washington, D. C. February, 1978.

Tibbitts, Clark. "Older Americans in the Family Context." Aging. Nos. 270-271. April/May, 1977.

Troll, Lillian, et al. Families in Later Life. Wadsworth Publishing Company, Inc. Belmont, California. 1979.

Weg, Ruth B. The Aged: Who, Where, How Well (Education, Health, Income, Marital Status). Virginia Office on Aging Training Session for College Faculty Teaching Courses in Gerontology. Williamsburg, Virginia. August, 1976.

Working With Older People: Vol. III. The Aging Person: Needs and Services. U. S. Department of Health, Education and Welfare. Public Health Service. U. S. Government Printing Office. Rockville, Maryland. 1970.

World Population Data Sheet, 1977. Population Reference
    Bureau, Inc. Washington, D. C.

III

OLDER AMERICANS LEGISLATION:
BRIGHT PROMISE OR FALSE HOPE

For many years, elderly citizens have received re-
cognition at the national and state levels in the form
of special dispensations, such as, double personal exemption at age 65 for Federal income tax, non-taxed
Social Security income, and, in some states, tax exemption for other pensions. These provisions were quietly
initiated and enacted, and they were applied equally to
all persons past a certain age, usually age 65. Such
statutory exemptions were routine. No effort was made
to pry into or meddle with individual lifestyles, levels
of income or personal assets. Instead, there was a
general public acceptance that the beneficiaries were
citizens who had made productive contributions to society
over long years, who had paid their property and school
taxes and had supported all levels of government, its
services and obligations. Now, in later life, these
older citizens were accorded considerations to which they
were justly due.

For elderly persons who lacked pension benefits, and
who, through misfortune, limited opportunity or irrespon-
sibility had not accumulated assets to cushion their
needs in old age, family, public welfare and private
philanthropy were expected to insure the necessities of
life. Admittedly, public provisions were sometimes
meager, and communities did not always give adequate
shelter and nurture to their elderly. Nonetheless, many
communities did assume responsibility for their own,

43

answering affirmatively by their deeds the question, "Am I my brother's keeper?".

As communities have grown, as the population has become more mobile, and as neighbors have become strangers to one another, the patterns of life and the interdependencies of people have changed. More and more official agencies have been delegated responsibility for those in need. This development has introduced a whole galaxy of implementing guidelines, procedural regulations, and a common usage of means tests as criteria for obtaining minimal necessities. It is increasingly evident that "government programs for older people seek to shift the responsibility for meeting some of their (the elderly's) needs from family to the various levels of government."[1] As assignment of responsibility for these old people began to move from the immediate and extended family to community, to state and then to the Federal government, such ingredients as human dignity, individualized service and personal obligations became the compromised victims of the transfers.[2] In retrospect, psychological stress and even physical suffering among the aged seem to have increased proportionately with the growth of the service bureaucracy as it moved further away from the individuals it was constructed to aid. The professional "helpers" did not have an emotional commitment to their "clients" built upon understandings bred through long continuity of relationships.

These conditions pertained until visibility of the old was enhanced in the sixties as the result of cumulative social changes. Not only were the elderly the fastest growing segment of the population, but the effects of inflation upon their security had become so pervasive they could no longer be ignored. A third set of parallel circumstances emphasized their non-essential role in society, namely, the national cult of youth worship that had evolved together with the mushroom growth of technology, in which young technicians were viewed as the finite key to the Nation's scientific and economic survival. This combination of interrelated forces assured the obsolescence of the elderly while, at the same time, their numbers continued to grow.

Relatively few voices had been raised during the second quarter of the twentieth century about older people and their needs, and concerted political action was minimal. In 1929, California was the first state to enact an old age assistance program, but this did not precipitate like action in other states. The Great

Depression spawned increased awareness of the financial plight of older workers, an awareness demonstrated by several movements that originated in California, the Upton Sinclair "End Poverty in California" (EPIC), the Utopian Society and the McLain Movement. It was, however, the Townsend Movement advocating a national pension system of $200 a month that is best known of these early organized efforts to achieve age-based pension legislation. This movement gained substantial national membership and attention, perhaps contributing to the passage of Social Security legislation in 1935.[3] More obscure and less well known are the early retirement plans of a few corporations as well as some labor union efforts.

After the Depression ended and Social Security had been inaugurated as a supplemental retirement income program, the growing number of older citizens received scant attention. Pockets of interest in aging and the aged were few, and the status and role of older Americans continued to erode. Not until the first National Conference on Aging organized by the Federal Security Agency in 1950 was there anything akin to national attention focused upon the increasing size of this segment of the population, at least to the extent of the 800 persons who attended.[4] Although recommendations resulted, serious attention to aging remained largely within limited academic circles and focused primarily upon gerontological research.

In 1961, the first White House Conference on Aging authorized by Congress and called by the President was convened in Washington with 2800 delegates representing the states and a number of organizations.[5] It was not until this meeting that a true national concerted attention was given to the aged in the United States. This Conference concentrated upon financial condition and needed health care services for the elderly, and upon specific recommendations for accomplishing the changes advocated. Within several years after this groundswell of attention to the older population, some of the Conference recommendations were implemented by legislated programs, most notable being increased Social Security benefits, and Medicare/Medicaid programs, and the Older Americans Act, all enacted in 1965.

The Older Americans Act created the Federal Administration on Aging together with its system of state agencies on aging. Additionally, it set forth 10 national objectives[6] of far-flung and sweeping intent:

45

1. An adequate retirement income for the American standard of living.
2. The best possible physical and mental health available regardless of economic status.
3. Suitable and freely selected housing to meet needs and economic status.
4. Full restorative services in care institutions.
5. Non-discriminatory employment.
6. Retirement in health, honor and dignity.
7. Full opportunities for pursuit of meaningful activities.
8. Efficient, coordinated community services that are readily available.
9. Immediate benefits from new knowledge to improve health and happiness.
10. Freedom and independence for free exercise of individual initiative in planning and managing one's own affairs.

In contrast with these noble and utopian objectives, however, were the specific bureaucratic functions assigned to the Administration on Aging. This agency, created by the Act to achieve the objectives, was directed to:[7]

1. Serve as a clearinghouse for information on problems of the aged and aging.
2. Assist the Secretary of HEW in matters concerning problems of the aged.
3. Administer grants provided in the Act.
4. Develop plans and conduct and arrange for research and demonstrations on aging.
5. Provide technical assistance to states and their political subdivisions on programs for the aged.
6. Prepare, publish and disseminate educational materials on welfare of the aged.
7. Gather statistics in the field of aging.
8. Stimulate more effective use of existing resources and services for the aged.

It seems evident that the functions assigned should not be expected to achieve the stated objectives.

To implement the Act, the initial enabling appropriation of $7,500,000 was authorized to begin three grant programs specified in the Act:[8]

(1) Title III provided monies to support state agencies on aging and for grants to non-profit public and private agencies and or-

organizations on a matching basis to be
used in community program development,
for new and expanded services, for
demonstration projects and for training
service personnel.

(2) Title IV gave to the Administration on
Aging authority to make both grants and
contracts for demonstration projects and
research determined to have regional or
national value, provided the projects
and investigations met established guidelines of acceptability.

(3) Title V gave to the Administration on
Aging authorization to make grants or
enter into contracts with non-profit
agencies or institutions for training
programs designed for employees in
programs and services for the aged.

Ir is interesting to note that the provisions for the new
Administration on Aging neither recommended nor required
that those administering and controlling the program have
qualifications in the field of their responsibility.

Actually, during the decade of the sixties, the lot
of older Americans was not greatly changed by this piece
of legislation, although appropriations increased and
competition for the grant dollars was keen. It was
widely reported that a large number of aged people lived
in dire poverty, an estimated one-fourth of that population, approximately 5 million persons.[9] At this point
it was evident that the objectives of the Older Americans Act had not been reached.

The Second White House Conference on Aging was convened in 1971, with initial funding by Congress of
$1,900,000 for Conference planning, implementation and
follow-up. The stated goal was to develop a national
policy on aging. Over 4500 delegates attended who
represented all the states and territories and several
hundred organizations. In addition there were a number
of domestic and foreign observers. A proliferation of
subjects was considered, related not only to the aged,
but also to the middle-aged. The deliberations and
recommendations that resulted were extensive and far
reaching and and these were summarized in a two volume
report.[10] The Post-White House Conference on Aging
Reports, 1973, encompassed not only the Administration's

response to the recommendations but also the final
report of the Post-Conference Board, a volume of 637
pages of small print.[11]

Following the 1971 Conference, one of the issues
drew accentuated attention, e.g., the nursing home
industry and elderly patients in nursing homes as well
as those in mental hospitals. The crusade that was
mounted to change existing conditions too often characterized by neglect and even mistreatment led to Federally
mandated licensure requirements. These requirements
included inspections, fire safety, dietary standards,
social services, medical supervision and other patient
protection tied increasingly to the Medicare/Medicaid
dollars that states sought.[12]

Other social and economic areas also were targeted
for Federal action following considerable publicity, and
the "plight" of the elderly became the cause célèbre in
the halls of Congress. Among these, but not limited to
them, were: (1) the extension of the Age Discrimination
Employment Act to the public sector (1971); (2) the
inauguration of a national nutrition program (1971) and
further expansion of it in 1974 (Title VII, OAA); (3)
initiation of an employment program (Title IX, OAA, 1973);
(4) the Pension Reform Bill to protect private pensions
(1974); (5) creation of the National Institute on
Aging (1974); (6) the elimination of mandatory retirement
at age 65 years (1978). One of the least publicized
actions following the Second White House Conference on
Aging was the establishment of a Standing Committee
charged with the duty of vigorously promoting legislation
and other actions that would implement the Conference
recommendations for all elderly citizens.[13] The result
has been expanding programs accomplished by a proliferation of amendments to old statutes, new legislation and
and new regulations on a wide variety of subjects.

Along with the new laws and their implementing regulations and procedures, there was developing a system of
multiple agencies and offices created to manage and
monitor all of the programs. Since the programs are
fragmented and uncoordinated, involving many different
departments and their component parts, the management
structure has reflected the growing pervasiveness of
their collective reach, e.g., housing, food distribution,
medical care, income, home maintenance, home health care,
recreation, housekeeping, fuel in winter, vacations in
summer, employment and transportation, to name only some
of the innovations instituted and funded under Federal

legislative provisions. All of these have not diminished
the grants and contracts to study, to investigate, to
demonstrate, which continue to support widening sectors
of academia and private enterprise consultant firms.

The change that has occurred is readily apparent
even in so cursory a review of the happenings in the
field of aging and in the Nation's relations with its
older citizens. The full impact of that change has not
yet been assessed, although more than a decade has passed
since it all began in the mid-sixties. Some assessment
of the quality of the change and its consequences seems
in order.

Role Assignment by Statute

Heightened general awareness of the older population
has grown in large measure as the result of publicized
investigative reports and Federal programs. The effects
of this enhanced awareness, however, have not always been
positive either among the general population or among the
elderly themselves. There is often sharp contrast between
the picture painted of millions of destitute, sick, mentally deteriorating, malnourished, lonely old people and
the high visibility of alert, active, involved, healthy,
elderly citizens. To the young, saddled with inflation,
high taxes, and escalating problems at home and abroad,
what they see becomes an added burden of growing numbers
of non-producers to be supported by ever increasing
Social Security assessments which still might not be
there for them thirty years later. To the old, also
struggling with inflation, social unrest and instability,
the image constitutes an added threat, not only to their
self image, but also as a "Sword of Damocles" menacing
their health and happiness, a possible omen of things to
come. These conditions have not fostered feelings of
hostility one to another yet, but they do not encourage
an atmosphere of mutual understanding and could bode
problems for the future.

Many of the reports that have been issued on the
health care and living conditions of elderly persons in
the United States have been concentrated on the sick in
nursing homes, and on those in the community whose resources are too little to provide even a minimally
adequate standard of living. Quite appropriately, these
findings have raised a public demand for change of the
conditions described. However, the nature of legislation

49

enacted to correct the difficulties identified has had
a psychological effect upon the public of magnifying
the extent and scope of the problem. Conditions that
actually affect a relatively small proportion of the
elderly often take on a global application to the total
older population, reinforcing the age old stereotype of
their incapacity, ineffectiveness and inability.

Although the 1965 Older Americans Act,[14] by its very
title as well as in its stated intent, purports to meet
diverse needs of a diverse elderly population of older
American citizens, it has two inherent weaknesses.

First, the Act designates age 60 as the chronological point when one may obtain its benefits, and,
therefore, this becomes the legislated entrance into old
age. This flies in the face of other Federally accepted
precedents for age 65 being the point at which specific
considerations are given to older citizens. For example,
at age 65 a person becomes eligible for a double personal
exemption for purposes of Federal income tax, eligible to
draw full retirement benefits from Social Security, and
eligible for Federal Medicare insurance. Despite all
these, the same Federal government concomitantly says
you are "old" at 60 years of age.

This legislated old age by assignment totally disregards the incongruity between the stated and implied
elevated purpose of the Act, namely, an open door to all
of the rights, privileges and responsibilities of full
citizenship for the elderly, and "the free exercise of
individual initiative in planning and managing their own
lives", with all needed supports and care available when
functional old age and changing circumstances shall indicate a need. By arbitrarily selecting age 60 as a
beginning point for being old, there has been a total
disregard for the fact that a high percentage of persons
between 60 and 64 years of age are productive wage
earners (65.7 per cent men and 33.3 per cent females in
the United States, 1975),[15] are not yet eligible for
private old age pensions nor for full benefits under
Social Security, and, indeed, do not regard themselves
as old. One man expressed it well when he commented,
"It came as a confusing shock to me at 60 to learn that
I was 'over the hill', while simultaneously receiving
notification that I had been promoted to a more responsible and demanding position."

The only purpose this arbitrary old age designation
of age 60 can serve is to inflate artificially the size

of the "aged" minority in order to obtain more impressive statistics to support higher appropriations. It must be extremely difficult for an advocacy agency, e.g., the Administration on Aging, to sell the productive capacity, competence and skills of older citizens while simultaneously mandated to label them as needing special benefits and supports solely on the basis of chronological age, even before a large segment are considering retirement. As further testimony to the fallacy in this conceptualization of aging, neither biologists nor physiologists find declining function to be a necessary concomitant of age 60,[16] a fact accepted recently when Congress acted to terminate compulsory retirement at age 65.

A second weakness in the Older Americans Act has been the fact that it is portrayed as age-entitlement legislation to benefit citizens age 60 and above, while its implementation has been most visible as poverty legislation. For example, Title VII, the Nutrition Program, and Title IX, Community Service Employment for Older Americans (Titles scheduled to become Sections of Title III in 1979) are two better publicized programs, both of which are targeted to the "low-income" aged with eligibility beginning at ages 60 and 55 respectively. In addition, social services specified under Title III also have been more applicable in the main to the old who are also poor and deprived. Other Titles which establish the Federal Office on Aging, the state and area offices, and provide for planning, training and research have less influence upon public conception of AOA programs than do the "welfare" components. As a result, the poverty thrust of the Older Americans Act is enhanced. Not until 1978 and the Ninety-fifth Congress, however, was the Older Americans Act specifically assigned the role of poverty legislation. It was then that the social service aspects were enlarged, and legislated priority services defined under the specific charge that these services must be provided only to those "in greatest economic and social need." It was then that the Older Americans Act officially became the Older Americans "Poverty" Act, but without name change.

In spite of the influence of this Act and its subsequent amendments in portraying the old as having ever heightening needs reflected in the mounting costs of meeting them, the total provisions of the Act actually have always benefited a relatively small proportion of the over 22 million aged persons in the United States. The legislation that has had and continues to have major

51

impact upon the total older population is the Social
Security Act of 1935 together with the Medicare Amendment to that Act in 1965.[17] Interestingly, these are
the two programs to which the beneficiaries have made,
and continue to make, money contributions. This point
seems important when evaluating the extent of the influence of escalating Federal programs for the aged as
well as in projecting anticipated cost-benefit relationship of such programs in the future. It also should
become increasingly difficult to assign a depreciated,
dependent role to so many millions of citizens who have
paid their way in society and continue to do so.

There also are several other ramifications of the
invidious emphasis upon negative social aspects of being
old and the need for government intervention. One is
the portrayal of the elderly as idle, inactive and
lonely. When one sees the dynamic symphony conductor
in his 80's, a traveler-researcher in his 70's, a
political leader or actress who is approaching the eighth
or ninth decade of life, the general reaction is that
this one is exceptional; he or she is different. Since
government paints a picture of "over the hill" for this
age group, it is more difficult to appreciate that there
are thousands of counterparts for the media-visible aged;
the majority are just less famous and less conspicuous.

Another repercussion is in the labor market. While
inacting an anti-discrimination law for age, the government concurrently advertises the plight of the old as sick,
frail and in need. The employer hears the latter, reinforcing his own negative feelings about old age, and the
older worker is penalized in job opportunities. Fortun-
ately or unfortunately, man's emotions cannot be legislated. Extending mandatory retirement age to 70 years
has little effect upon this stereotype, since what is done
has far greater impact than what is said.

A third insidious effect is related to the government emphasis upon activity, getting involved with
recreational programs, being physically and socially
mobile, being "on-the-go" regardless of purpose. In
younger years one may be an introvert or an extrovert,
but in old age all are supposed to be gregarious, socially
active and involved in games, crafts or leisure time pur-
suits. And so, with government financial assistance to
government programs, the old are perceived as idle folks
to be amused while a younger generation works to support
them. The fact that it is only a small minority of the
elderly who attend senior centers or other aged group

52

programs is not advertised.

Through working with older citizens and especially by listening to them, it becomes apparent that they do not want to be assigned a late life role. They wish to live life to its end exactly as they want to live it. In fact, they show no enthusiasm for the government protecting them from themselves, even raising serious questions about their ability to afford the inflationary cost of this government intervention and interference.

It seems appropriate here to ask, what is the intent of the Federal government toward elderly citizens? What value standards are in effect? In the absence of any National policy on aging in America, is it possible to achieve at least an ethical consistency in attitude and in treatment of the old? Is it conceivable that some old people of unlike economic circumstances may have common social needs, or that those of like economic conditions may have vastly different perceptions of their needs? Is it, in fact, really necessary to assign old age, or might it not occur as a natural and variable phenomenon of an individual life?

Rediscovery of the Dole

Persons now regarded as elderly were born at the turn of the century, just before the end of the nineteenth century or in the early years of the twentieth. They were reared in the culture of the Victorian era, not in a time of paternalistic government of socialistic beliefs. They have strong emotional value ties to a traditional national philosophy of fierce independence, individual self-determination, and equality premised in open doors to opportunity, with a personal responsibility for achieving it. They survived the Great Depression with an even stronger devotion to the importance of work and to moneyed independence.

It is against this background of basic beliefs that Federal programs pertaining to the elderly have been enacted, modified, revised and amended. With consummate consistency, changes have reinforced negative stereotypes of old age. Before all the changes, negativism toward being old had been largely attitudinal, a cultural heritage, but now it is legislated and given the status of law. A few examples will illustrate the point.

Social Security*

    In 1935, a person derived retirement supplementary
income from Social Security based upon length of employment in a covered occupation and upon "contributions" to
the plan. Wages up to $3,000 a year were taxed, and for
the majority this was also their total wages. It was
simply a pension plan for workers administered by the
government.Very quickly, the Act was expanded to include
dependents who survived the deceased worker, and there
was a small death benefit. A key point to remember is
that Social Security, as initiated, was a program of retirement income made possible by the worker's own
"contributions" matched by those of his employer.

    In 1950, Congress enacted the first major amendment
to the Social Security Act. Then the benefits were
adjusted, the wage base was increased to $3,600, the tax
to 1.5 per cent, and coverage was broadened to include
millions of jobs previously excluded, e.g., household
employees, farm workers and a substantial percentage of
self-employed persons. Between then and 1967 benefits
were increased five times, tax rates increased eight
times, and the wage base three times. Paralleling these

Table 11

Maximum Taxable Earnings, Tax Rates and Maximum Tax Levied
1954 - 1967

Year	Maximum Taxable Earnings	Tax Rate[a] Per Cent	Maximum[a] Tax Levied
1954	$ 3600	2.0	$ 72.00
1955	4200	2.0	84.00
1957	4200	2.25	94.50
1959	4800	2.5	120.00
1960	4800	3.0	144.00
1962	4800	3.125	150.00
1963	4800	3.625	174.00
1966	6600	4.2	277.20
1967	6600	4.4	290.40

[a] Employee and employers each paid this rate.
Source of data: Social Security Administration.

* Historical data concerning the Social Security System,
  both the original Act and subsequent amendments, are
  documented in the General References of this chapter.

tax rate and base changes were subsequent coverage extensions to most of the self-employed not previously included, members of the Armed Forces, and the option of coverage extended to employees of state and local governments. When these beneficiaries were added to those covered by the Federal Civil Service Retirement System and the Railroad Retirement Board, the coverage had reached approximately 95 per cent of the Nation's wage earners.

Expansion of workers covered and increased benefits were not the only changes legislated in the series of amendments from the fifties and into the sixties. Benefits also were extended to children of deceased and retired workers, to dependent parents of deceased workers, to all persons who did not have a sufficient number of calendar quarters of work in covered employment to be eligible, and early retirement at age 62 was inaugurated for women. In 1961, the option of early retirement at age 62 for men was added in response to a high unemployment. Other expansions included benefits for workers under 65 who were disabled or in poor health.

Even with these changes, however, the program still had a potential for solvency. Then, in 1965, the Medicare Health Insurance for the elderly (65 and above) was added as Title XVIII of the Social Security Act, including both hospital and medical care provisions, with costs to be shared by the individuals and the Federal government. Departing even further from the original philosophy of the Social Security Act was Title XIX, Medicaid, a program of health care assistance for medically indigent persons of all ages, a welfare program. It was the 1965 amendments that actually finalized the change in the institution of Social Security from its original intent and purpose. Heretofore, changes and expansions had been mainly in the context of insured and earned retirement income benefits. This now was changed.

In 1972, in order to fund a 20 per cent increase in benefits, a hike in taxes was made that would raise the Social Security tax rate to 5.85 per cent on $10,800 wages in 1973 and escalate to 6.05 per cent on $17,700 by 1978, accompanied, of course, by a substantial bounty of benefits. This means that the total employee-employer tax became 12.10 per cent in 1978, or a total of $2141.70 on the ceiling wage, more than tripling the tax within five years.

Among the new expanded provisions to be borne by
the "retirement fund" were not only an automatic cost-of-
living increase based upon the Consumer Price Index and
larger widows' benefits, but also added were the ponder-
ous burdens of: (1) further liberalization of eligibility rules; (2) extension of the Medicare health insurance to include younger adults who were either disabled or had chronic kidney disease, including the cost
of dialysis; and (3) administration of the welfare program of Supplementary Security Income for the elderly.
At this point, an earned employee-employer financed retirement pension system was melded with the adult welfare
program for the aged, blind and disabled and they became
one.

More recently, in 1978, other strains were legislated
for the Social Security Trust by expanding still further
the benefits and beneficiaries of its funds, despite the
admittedly serious financial problems in the Social
Security System. Beginning in 1979, the payroll tax and
the earning ceiling for taxation will rise annually until
1987 when it is legislated to reach 7.15 per cent on
earnings up to $42,600.

Table 12

Legislated Projected Changes in Social Security Wage Base,
Tax and Maximum Worker Cost, 1978 - 1987.

Year	Taxable Wage	Tax Rate	Maximum Tax
1978	$ 17,700	6.05 %	$ 1,070.85
1979	22,900	6.13	1,403.77
1980	25,900	6.13	1,587.67
1981	29,700	6.65	1,975.05
1982	31,800	6.70	2,130.60
1983	33,900	6.70	2,271.30
1984	36,000	6.70	2,412.00
1985	38,100	7.05	2,686.05
1986	40,200	7.15	2,874.30
1987	42,600	7.15	3,045.90

Source of data: The Social Security Administration.

Among changes to be supported by the escalating
taxation are: (1) a widow 60 years of age or older can
still draw benefits derived from her deceased husband's

work even if she has remarried, and (2) a divorced wife
who had been married as long as 10 years (a change from
the previously designated 20 years) can draw both death
and retirement benefits on her former husband's work
record. These provisions go beyond the already well
established policy of regressive payroll taxes to finance
a Federal welfare program while continuing the now dis-
honest practice of calling Social Security a workers'
retirement program. At this point, it would appear that
the government is supporting "financial bigamy" and
supporting, even encouraging, the institution of divorce.
Certainly there is documented evidence that there are
instances where women in each of the above categories
have financial problems. The question is whether the
Federal Government is supposed to solve every citizen's
private problems under the guise of a worker supported
retirement program for workers.

   Although not comprehensive, this sequence of events
shows clearly that, during the period of growing attention
to older citizens, Social Security benefits have not only
been improved to reflect changing economic conditions
characterized by rising wage levels, but changes have gone
far beyond reasonable alterations for that purpose. The
fund created as an employee-employer financed supplementary pension system for workers now has become a welfare
dispersal agent for persons completely outside the original intent of this Federal pension plan. In the confusion that has been legislatively created and adminis-
tratively supported, those who have purchased this security are deriving an ever decreasing percentage of the
benefits, while more and more beginning to look like a
part of the welfare recipient population as lines of
demarcation are eradicated.

   A further condition given almost no attention is
that a single wage earner pays into the system the same
contribution as a married worker while the married worker beneficiaries derive an excessive amount of the benefits, and these benefits continue to mount. It is broadly
estimated that 25 per cent of persons in the United
States aged 65 years and over live in "near poverty"
(125 per cent of the poverty threshold which in 1975 was
$4,040 for couples and $3,215 for individuals) and 15 per
cent below the poverty line (couples $3,232 and indivi-
duals $2,572).[18] The individual aged represented a dis-
proportionate number of those at either level in 1975,
an estimated 8 per cent of older couples but 31 per cent
of elderly individuals falling into the poverty category,
and with even wider variations by sex and race.[19] Further

57

demonstrating the economic status difference between
couples and individuals is the fact that 7 per cent of
families 65 and over had annual incomes under $3,000
while 8 per cent of individuals had less than $1,500;
one-third of families had incomes under $6,000, but
individuals with incomes between $1,500 and $3,000
brought the total individuals under $3,000 to 42 per
cent.[20]

Both the 1975 and 1978 Social Security monthly payments for persons aged 65 and over also illustrate this
difference:

Monthly Social Security Payments to Persons 65 Years +	1975	1978
Single - minimum payment	$ 101.40	$ 121.80
Single - maximum payment	341.70	489.70
Average payment	205.18	254.00
Couple - minimum payment	152.10	182.70
Couple - maximum payment	512.60	733.60
Average payment	309.61	433.00

Source: Social Security Administration.

According to the Social Security Administration in 1974,
"The proportions at very low income levels are much higher
for the nonmarried than the married even when account is
taken of differential need."[21] A relevant question may
be, why has such extensive attention been given to expanding the rolls of dependent beneficiaries of the
Federal retirement system before giving adequate attention to the worker beneficiaries themselves and their
relative contributions, and to the differing protections
derived from these contributions? A fair and equitable
return on investment seems a reasonable arrangement between worker citizens and their government.

Among inequities that demand correction are: (1)
establishment of a positive relationship between length
of time and extent of "contribution" to benefits derived;
(2) the worker payment-worker benefit orientation versus
the dilution of worker benefits to support non-workers
and dependents of other workers; (3) worker purchased
equity in the system versus beneficiaries who are non-
contributors; (4) enforced support by contributing workers to welfare programs and non-eligible beneficiaries;
(5) the penalizing of 65-year-old workers who continue
to work while paying full benefits to peers who do not;

and (6) the basic dishonesty of dissipating the trust
fund through capricious mismanagement and disbursements
guaranteed to bankrupt a program initiated as a supplementary retirement income, and never conceived to achieve
"social adequacy" for all citizens and under all circumstances.

Earned pensions and welfare programs are historically
different, a difference which has logical justification.
Today, elderly citizens are being belittled and depreciated by a "dole" psychology after conscientiously participating in a dignified retirement pension program
during their long years of work. In brief, the concept
of insured income for one's old age has given way to
worker taxation for assured income for all.

Nutrition Program

Another example of the "dole" psychology that per-
meates programs for the aged is the nutrition program.
Here the approach is both beneficent and custodial.

Two conditions affecting a large percentage of
elderly persons, according to self-appointed and largely
uninformed advocates for the aged, are loneliness and
issolation, with a third and related condition being
inadequate diet and malnutrition. To solve this composite problem, a national nutrition program for the elderly
was inaugurated in 1972 as an amendment to the Older
Americans Act of 1965.[22] Under the provisions of the
then new Title VII, need would be met for "low cost,
nutritionally sound meals served in strategically located"
congregate settings. Additionally, transportation would
be furnished to the sites when needed as well as delivery
of meals to older persons confined to their homes. Major
emphasis, however, has been given to group sites located
conveniently for fairly high concentrations of older low
income persons.

Also specified in the Title VII Amendment was that
charges for meals would be made "pursuant to guidelines
established by the Commissioner" on Aging. In accordance with this legislated provision, "Rule and Regulations" for administration of the nutrition program,
published in the Federal Register,[23] include the statement that opportunity would be provided "for the participants in nutrition projects to pay all or part of the
costs of the meals" and that "schedules of suggested
fees" would be established. However, regulations also
stated that age eligible individuals would pay according

to their means as determined by themselves, and no one would be denied participation because of inability to pay. In practice, since no one can be required to pay anything, project incomes have continued to be negligible.

In order to "socialize" the elderly persons who attend, it is mandated that recreational and informational programs, and social services as needed, be carried out in conjunction with the serving of meals. In short, it would appear that each participant is expected to make a non-money payment by playing games, singing, listening to lectures, being entertained, or being instructed in some aspect of his life. These costs, of course, are an integral part of the program budgets.

Since, according to the implementing regulations for the program, each site is to be located not only where there is a density of population over 60 years of age but also with priority given to serving those below a prescribed income level, some inconsistencies emerge. If two purposes of this program are to combat loneliness and lessen isolation, it appears that government's concern is primarily for those lonely, isolated and also poor, with largely a cavalier disregard for the fact that persons not living in poverty also can be lonely and isolated. In fact, the often crowded living conditions of the very poor could result in less isolation rather than more. Insofar as teaching elderly persons what to eat is concerned (education being one of the identified goals of the nutrition program), there is little likelihood that eating patterns established over 60 or 70 years will be changed, and, if their food choices have not killed these older people so far, there is a good chance life long eating habits were not hazardous to their health.

Visits to some of the nutrition sites for the lonely and isolated elderly poor quickly demonstrate that those attending, at least in these locations, are largely persons who are already socially active, and this is just one more activity added to their others. Moreover, studies do not support the apparent conviction in official and legislative circles that a major problem of the old is loneliness. According to the aged themselves, far more concern is directed toward an adequate income and maintenance of health with its associated independence. Based upon the Harris Survey[24] findings, loneliness is reported to be a problem for 12 per cent of the over 65 age population, with a range from 10 per cent of the 65-69 age group to 17 per cent of those over 80 years.

This is a prevalence only approximately five per cent greater than in the general population between the ages of 18 and 64 years. Indications are that sex and education seem to be relevant factors affecting loneliness in all age groups, with females and those with less education having a larger problem.

One further consideration is the actual extent of the benefits derived from the Nutrition Program for both individual participants and for the older population as a whole. For example, in one area agency where the operational cost for this program is said to be the lowest in that state, the 1977-78 budget was approximately $588,000. For this amount, slightly more than 740 on-site and delivered meals were served each week in 23 locations at an average cost of $2.25 for each meal. This is in a service area with approximately 57,000 who are 65 years of age and over, and almost 26,000 persons between the ages of 60 and 64 years, who also were eligible for the program. The total cost of serving these meals was almost $800 for the year for each of 740 full time equivalent participants, or not quite one per cent of the age eligible persons in the service area. Since the program served an average of 240 days a year (which excludes weekends and holidays), each full time participant had a meal for approximately 66 per cent of the year, or roughly the equivalent of eight months.

On the other hand, were each of 740 elderly individuals provided an additional $800 a year in income, he could have had a comparable meal for 355 days, or roughly 97 per cent of the year. An important aspect of the situation regarding extent of benefit is that some 49 per cent of the program costs was consumed in management and operations, including overhead site costs, transportation, activities and related non-food expenditures. Because of Federal and State regulations concerning required staffing and operational procedures, the costs are higher than necessary. Another factor is mandated waste of unused food. If a site has prepared for 50 persons and only 25 appear to eat, there are instances where it has been required that the on-site uneaten meals, with the exception of bakery items and fresh fruit, be discarded. This food cannot legitimately be given to those present to take home for another meal, even when the nutrition site is in the same building in which some of the participants live. It is such examples as this that give the impression that government interest in nutrition for the elderly may be less strong than is its devotion to regulating them.

61

Yet another factual condition appears to belie the Federal assumption that the old people served by their nutrition program are frail, isolated and malnourished as the result of their inability to function effectively. If this were true, why is it reported in both urban and rural locations that attendance drops in the Spring when the weather is good? One reason given is that older people are busy with outdoor chores, such as planting their gardens. This lends at least reasonable credance to the suggestion that the Nutrition Program designed for the many may be something needed by a few who could be much better served differently.

In support of the idea of the relative few rather than the many who either need or use the program is the report by a Federal official in late 1978,[25] which stated that 1074 nutrition programs in the Nation utilized 9732 meal sites to serve an average of 467,000 meals daily. Of this number, 17 per cent (79,390) were home delivered. This means that only a negligible number of the elderly in the entire United States were participating in this program, and experience has demonstrated that not all of these are aged poor. One can only hazard a guess as to what the nutritional benefits might have been had 467,000 of the truly poor elderly, approximately 10 per cent, received an increase in annual income of $600, all of which could have been spent for food.

It should be noted, too, that those who receive home delivered meals have other needs, making this a question-able benefit for other than a selective few whose incapac-ity is of limited severity and duration. They need more interaction with people than the brief contact with the meal deliverer; they need shopping for other things in addition to some for food; they need laundry and cleaning, to name only several of the necessities of life outside the one hot meal and a cold snack. For at least some of the individuals receiving home delivered meals, better solutions to dealing with their frailty should be sought.

In contrast with the Food Stamp Program, participa-tion in the Nutrition Program is based upon age entitle-ment rather than need entitlement, although site loca-tions and solicited attendance emphasize service to the elderly poor. There is, however, no firm evidence that Title VII has consistantly served either the needy or the malnourished. Nonetheless, the program costs have risen[26] rapidly from 125 million dollars in Fiscal Year 1975 to 200 million in 1976, 250 million in 1977, and 275 million in 1978.[27] With increased appropriations, the

number of sites also has been increased, and aggressive
solicitation for participants has been carried out in
conformity with published regulations (Federal Register,
Report II, August 19, 1972).

Despite all the efforts and the escalated funding,
it was reported that "approximately one per cent of the
eligible population is presently served by the Nutrition
Program authorized under the Older Americans Act of 1965,
21 per cent of whom are minority group members."[28] This
seems particularly pertinent in view of the estimated 15
per cent of older persons reported to be living below
the Federally defined poverty level.

Although the above evaluation of the limited reach
of the Nutrition Program was reported to Congress, the
1978 Senate-House Conferees agreed in Committee to
authorize funding for three years for "Congregate Nutrition" and "Home Delivered Meals" as follows:[29]

House-Senate Conference Bill, OAA (in millions)

	FY 1979	FY 1980	FY 1981
Congregate Nutrition	350	375	400
Home Delivered Nutrition	80	100	120
Totals	430	475	520

Although the Ninety-Fifth Congress adjourned before the
Appropriations bill was enacted, the above funding levels
are expected to prevail in the Ninety-Sixth Congress.
This means that between 1975 and 1981 the Nutrition Program appropriations will have gone from 125 million
dollars to 520 million, a 316 per cent increase in seven
years. If these latter appropriations are passed as expected, the total expenditures for the Nutrition Program
for the elderly will be in excess of two billion dollars
in only seven years. And this without any clear-cut knowledge of what these vast expenditures have produced in
measurable benefits to elderly citizens.

One small illustration of bloated costs as well as
the level of receptivity for the Nutrition Program among
the aged can be found in a short term outreach effort
that occurred in one community in 1977. This project was
funded by a $13,190 grant under Title VII in accordance
with the Federal mandate to locate low income participants.[30] Eight outreach workers sought to locate elderly
persons 60 years of age and over who could not afford to

eat adequately, lacked skills and/or knowledge to select and/or prepare nourishing meals, had limited mobility to shop and cook, and felt rejected and lonely. Transportation to the nutrition sites would be provided. At the end of the 10-week crash effort, 1,044 "eligible" individuals had been contacted and 150 agreed to attend. Another 67 said they would do so when sites at new locations should become available, bringing the total to 217 persons, slightly less than 21 per cent, who agreed to participate. If all who agreed actually did so (and this is improbable), this exercise in persuasion cost approximately $61 for each of those persuaded. Reasons cited for not taking part in the program by the 827 who refused included: did not have time, health reasons, caring for a disabled spouse, baby sitting, summer heat, summer activities, and lack of interest.

The questions such a report raises are many, both with regard to the worth of the funded projects and the actual level and extent of the assumed need. There is no doubt that these 1,044 individuals had problems, but it must be questioned whether the problems were the simplistic ones implied and whether their incompetence to deal with their problems was as great as described.

Such isolated incidences do not define either success or failure of a program, but may serve to illustrate the hazards of over-zealous advocacy supported more by available money than by reasoned common sense.

It remains a fact that there are numerous older people who look askance at government gifts. Because the Nutrition Program meals carry no price tag, the reaction of some potential participants is negative. The "free" label causes many who are in the low income category and actually need financial assistance to boycott the perceived "charity" programs. The contrived socialization component, being told how to eat and to live, also invites some to compare it to a kindergarten and to reject it. At least in a sample of communities, the most aggressive campaigns to solicit participation have produced minimal results among proud elderly people.

There is a minority of older persons in the United States who need a great deal of assistance of various kinds, while there is a far greater number who need more adequate incomes. It is equally true that the nutrition projects reach relatively few in either group. There also exists a strong probability that those with special needs can be served better by freely initiated services established by their communities in accordance with the differing cultures and life styles that are a primary characteristic of the heterogeniety of the Nation of which they are a part.

Means Test Programs

A final example of the "dole" influence in programs for the aged is the means test. There are a host of Federal need entitlement programs which require that recipients of services and benefits document their lack of financial self-sufficiency to cope with their basis requirements. Among these programs for which elderly citizens may qualify are: food stamps and surplus commodities, public housing and housing subsidies, Medicaid, Supplementary Security Income, home health and housekeeper aides, fuel relief, home maintenance and chore services, home winterization, and Federally funded employment. Even participation in such volunteer programs as Foster Grandparents, Green Thumb and Green Light have eligibility criteria tied to economic status. Furthermore, these programs are administered by a variety of Federal departments and agencies, each with different regulations, procedures and requirements for participation.

So strong is the pride of many elderly persons, however, that they prefer doing without the proffered assistance rather than "begging" help. Magnifying their embarrassment is the necessity to declare their poverty repetitively in order to qualify for different services, e.g., food, housing, medical care, et al. The price they must pay in self esteem and privacy can be too great.

Since the initiation of such Federal programs there has been a contamination influence at the state level. For example, an elderly person usually cannot obtain tax relief in the form of reduced real estate taxes on his home unless he proves that both his net worth and his annual income are below an established maximum, and these ceilings can be quite low. In fact, the maximum annual income that permits property tax relief has been set at such a minimal level in some communities that it guarantees a relative few will be eligible. This is true even though some of those with incomes and net worth that preclude their taking this tax advantage will not have adequate incomes for a reasonably comfortable standard of living after they have paid their property taxes. Illustrating this are several examples of differing eligibility

requirements in adjacent communities where real estate
tax increases for homes have ranged as high as 130 per
cent within a one year period. In all of these instances, age 65 is an eligibility criterion.

Financial Worth Excluding Home	Preceding Year's Total Household Income	Excluded Income **	Type Community
$ 35,000	$ 10,000	$ 4,000	Urban
16,000	6,500	2,500	Rural
20,000 *	7,500	1,500	Suburban
12,000 *	4,000	1,200	Rural
20,000 *	7,500	2,500	Rural
25,000 *	6,750	2,400	Suburban

* Excluding home and one acre of land.
** Amount of excluded income for previous year for relatives living
    in home other than owner and spouse.

Given the accelerated increase in value of land and
buildings and the constantly rising economic inflation
now prevalent, even limited financial resources for
meeting unexpected or catastrophic emergencies can serve
to disqualify an individual for property tax relief.
Without this benefit, the result is that one's usable
income may be reduced in some cases to below the Federally defined poverty or near-poverty thresholds after he
has paid his taxes.

By definition, the word "dole" means to give out
sparingly or in small quantities, such as, money, food,
or other items, another name for ungenerous charity.
The programs now in effect for older persons in the
United States fit this description perfectly. Congress
has assumed the cloak of benefactor in doling out public
funds with the same noblesse oblige that, in former times,
was characterized by a lady bountiful dispensing her
charity from a food basket. The difference is that the
charity of an individual "doing good" incurred no over-
head expenses, while the complex and fragmented bureaucracy consumes millions of the "benefit" dollars in administrative costs.

By order of Congress in the 1973 Amendments to the
Older Americans Act, the Federal Council on Aging was
directed to "undertake a study of the interrelationships
of benefit programs for the elderly operated by Federal,
State, and local government agencies." It was further

directed that, following this study, the President was
to "submit to Congress recommendations for bringing
about greater uniformity of eligibility standards, and
for eliminating the negative impact that one program's
standards may have on another." This Federal Council
report, dated December 29, 1975, was duly submitted.[31]
According to the report of the House Education and Labor
Committee that accompanied the 1973 Amendments to the
Older Americans Act, the programs specified for attention were: Social Security, veterans benefits, old age
assistance, Medicare, Medicaid, low rent public housing,
Federally assisted private housing, food stamps, and
manpower training.[32]

The Federal Council study concentrated upon those
programs requiring income and/or asset tests and criteria for eligibility. Among findings reported were:

1. Very little concern for the relationship
   among programs.
2. Administrative complexity and expense.
3. Inequities in distribution of benefits
   and eligibility requirements.
4. Great divergence between planned and
   actual impact.
5. Tangled mix of benefits, including cash,
   food, housing, medical care and a
   long list of services. (p. 1)

Gross deficiencies and inequities were identified in the
application of both income and asset tests among several
programs and different agencies, as well as the variable
participation rates for some of the programs.

The report pointed out that, "for many programs designed to aid the elderly, the receipt of benefits is a
privilege rather than a right." All of the housing programs and the various programs under the Older Americans
Act fall into this "privileged" category. (Example given
was the Rent Supplement Program.) A conclusion reached
was that "....only a privileged few get any benefits from
this type of program." (p. 47) In this critical look
at a limited number of the Federal and Federal-State programs that impact upon older citizens, the obvious conclusion is that they are a hodge-podge of inconsistencies,
inequities, overlapping jurisdictions, excessive layers
of administration and exaggerated costs. Although this
information was released almost four years ago, the conditions described still pertain.

In a report released in 1976 by the National Council on the Aging,[33] yet another means test program was
reviewed. This program, Title XX, is a 1974 social
services amendment to the Social Security Act which became effective in 1975. It is designed to provide
Federally financed services on a 75/25 per cent Federal/
State match, and is administered by the States within
specific requirements by Federal authorities. Some
Title XX services that are most applicable to the elderly, such as, day care for adults, homemaker services,
home delivered and congregate meals, legal services,
transportation and senior centers, readily call to mind
provisions of the Older Americans Act as well.

There are many examples that can be offered to show
the confusion created when numerous Congressional Committees design independent programs that are uncoordinated with those already existing, and are implemented
by autonomous administrations and regulations.

Summary. In all of the programs specifically serving the aged and those available to include service to
the aged, participation by this segment of the population
varies from substantial to limited. The complexities
of means tests constitute both a problem of mechanics
for utilization and a moral dilemma for many of the
would be recipients of goods and services. The one known
factor in this whole construction of governmental hier-
archies is that millions of dollars in expenses are
involved which benefit only those who manage the programs.

Perhaps this "dole" psychology has connotations
more far ranging than are yet perceived. Can it be that
the few accorded the responsibility of representing over
200,000,000 citizens have also acquired such vast power
and privilege that they now view themselves as a ruling
class with authority to control rather than to represent?
If this is so, paternalism for the old can be only a
precursor of rule by oligarchy for all.

In Sickness and in Health

Despite the rather commonly held belief that "old"
and "sick" are synonymous, this is not true. Being sick
is not a normal or natural state at any age, including

68

old age. Admittedly, older persons have more chronic disabilities, e.g., arthritis, hearing and vision impairments, cardiac ailments, than does the younger population, while, in contrast, they also have fewer acute illnesses. With adequate medical surveillance and proper preventive care, it is reasonable to expect that most elderly persons have a potential for healthy lives.

Although health maintenance is a primary concern among older persons themselves, as well as a basic determinant of the quality of life in the later years, the availability of skilled geriatric medical resources has continued to be almost totally lacking in the United States. As the number of persons growing old steadily increases and the proportion of those living into very old age accelerates, this problem has now reached the status of a critical unmet need in the area of basic necessities.[34] Contributing to this situation and impeding solution to an obvious problem are several restrictive forces that have appeared to be distinguished by their intransigent immutability.

The Health Professions. The fundamental attitude in the health field towards aging and the aged is essentially fatalistic, with decrements in physical and mental function considered to be inevitable and irreversible. Not only are being old and sick considered normal, but, in fact, old age is regarded by many in the health field as a disease, an irremediable ailment. Since medicine is dedicated to the cure or alleviation of illness, and since old age cannot be cured, persons with this "disability" constitute an affront to medical skill. They make most medical practitioners uncomfortable, and, as a result, receive the same avoidance as do other "terminal" illnesses. Regardless of what the complaint may be, the response is, "What do you expect? You are old." The consequence is a lack of intensive investigation of the old patient's health condition and, at best, administration of palliative symptomatic treatment. Some physicians even refuse to accept elderly persons as patients.[35]

There is a chain reaction to this attitude, and the medical model conditions the therapeutic benefits available for old people from all of the allied health professions, e.g., physical, occupational and other therapies, nursing, pharmacy, to name several. Having made a judgment that their treatment is a waste of skill and time, elderly patients too often are consigned to medical neglect, not infrequently to unnecessary suffering and invalidism.[36]

One primary reason behind this circumstance is the failure of schools in the United States that train medical doctors and other health professionals to include training in the treatment of geriatric patients. This is perhaps the only age group essentially ignored in the training of health professionals. In 1973, a pre-medical student seeking preparation for practicing geriatric medicine found that in the some 94 medical schools in the United States at that time only a dozen had elective courses in geriatrics, and most of these were in departments of psychiatry. He was shocked to find that he could not prepare to be a geriatric specialist in any medical school in the entire United States.[37]

More recently, in 1976, Dr. Robert N. Butler, Director of the National Institute on Aging, testified before the Senate Special Committee on Aging that there were 32 elective courses in geriatric medicine in the 114 medical schools in the country. The competency of even these courses had to be in doubt, however, when he gave an estimate of fewer than 15 faculty qualified to teach geriatric medicine from the more than 25,000 medical school faculty members in the United States. He further reported that there was not one endowed chair in geriatric medicine in the Nation (now one at Cornell Medical Center in New York City established in 1978). This condition pertains in the United States despite the fact that geriatrics has long been a recognized medical specialty in other countries. For example, there are 10 endowed chairs of geriatric medicine in the United Kingdom, two in Sweden, and one in the little country of Holland.[38]

It becomes evident that even this minimal increase in attention by medicine to the fastest growing segment of the population is not an unmixed blessing. In view of the almost total absence of qualified teachers of geriatric medicine, expansion of course offerings presents other problems. Instruction by uninformed and incompetent teachers based upon old stereotypes and myths could be worse than none at all, since it would give false information the status of finite truth. It is an interesting commentary that, for years, monies have been generously available from both Federal and private sources for medical education and medical research, and how little of the benefits of it have accrued to elderly persons. Research funds for achieving prolongation of life have been

70

liberal, while minimal attention has been focused upon improving the quality of the life prolonged.[39]

Basic to the problem of competent, understanding medical treatment is the learned denigration of the elderly in health field training programs at all levels. In 1968, a report on medical student attitudes toward old patients stated that senior medical student attitudes did not improve over those of freshmen, but, in fact, actually deteriorated.[40] Obviously, such negativism can lead to discrimination against health care needs of old patients by medical practitioners. While the general public is using such palliative benign terms as "senior citizens" or "oldsters," medical students and their colleagues in auxiliary health occupations continue to refer to the aged sick as "old crocks," "old bags," "old fogeys," or worse, as anyone associated with medical training institutions can confirm. In short, all of society's negative stereotypes of aging are reinforced and taught in the health professions.

Research on Aging. The literature is filled with reports of investigative studies on why living organisms age and why certain deteriorative changes occur. Large volumes can be compiled of the reports on physiological changes in aging guinea pigs, monkeys, pigs, hamsters, birds, mosquitoes, chickens, dogs, house flies, microscopic organisms, and many more volumes on aging mice and rats. There are also studies on human aging. Much more limited are studies concerned with maintaining health and and function throughout a long life while living with the deteriorative effects of aging. This situation continues despite the direct applicability of advances that have been made in treatment and rehabilitative techniques that are fully appropriate for elderly persons when utilized for them with the same immediacy and intensity as for those in younger aged groups.

During the last decade especially, millions of Federal dollars have been appropriated for research on aging and for pilot and demonstration programs, not only in physical aspects but also in psychological and social ramifications of growing old. Voluminous reports attest to the studies. For the most part, however, the areas of investigation have been those of greatest interest to theoretical researchers, with a much smaller portion of the investment dedicated to the practical applicability of knowledge gained for the enhanced well being of those already old. Certainly, theoretical and applied research are not mutually exclusive. In fact, in the area of

71

health the latter should be a natural outgrowth of new knowledge available.[41] There is substantial evidence, however, that studying the elderly has become, for many, an end-product in itself, a popular diversion with degree of interest premised in the availability of funding. In fact, from much of this so-called research activity, the greatest benefit derived has been the economic benefit to the researchers who were funded. Support for this view is found in the many instances where interest in the aged has lasted only as long as did the Federal grants, along with the undeniable fact that availability and adequacy of health care and health maintenance for older persons has changed little as a result of the monies expended.

The Sick Aged. Federal programs in the health area have been concentrated upon maintaining the sick rather than either restoration of health or aggressive use of available therapies to improve function. Even less attention has been given to prevention of illness and of its handicapping consequences. Substantial legislation has been directed toward upgrading the sanitation, safety and management of nursing homes, including mandated social services, activities, medical oversight, food quality, among other considerations. Much less attention has gone to getting older persons out of nursing homes with their function improved through intensive therapeutic measures. In contrast, nursing home patients receive very little medical attention and essentially no rehabilitative medical supervision and surveillance. Physicians' visits are infrequent, and often amount to nothing more than a "walk through" of momentary duration per patient followed by a renewal of sedative drugs for the benefit of the staff.

Home care during convalescence following an acute illness or for maintenance of function when the disability is chronic is sparsely provided under both the Medicare and Medicaid programs, although the potential benefit to the patient can be great and it is admittedly cost effective. The number of home visits is limited by Medicare, and, although a limit to the number of visits is not specified under Medicaid, both extent and availability of service is within the authority of the individual states, and many physicians do not even prescribe this care for their elderly patients. Under the Medicare program, less than one per cent of the total Medicare funds expended in 1975 were for home health care,[42] and this percentage has remained constant for several years. These limits and restrictions mean that older persons

received medical attention for acute illness, but, in
large measure, lack follow up and continuity of care
needed to achieve restoration to their maximum health
potential. The result is that, lacking necessary medical supervision and nursing care after the acute phase
of illness, fullest recovery possible is not achieved
and vulnerability to another serious illness is enhanced.

Nowhere is the fundamental depreciating attitude
toward the elderly better demonstrated than in the treatment of the sick aged, or perhaps more accurately stated,
the mistreatment. Not only are they often neglected and
denied the quality and intensity of care provided those
of younger years, but they are victimized by those committed to do them no harm. Pharmaceutical companies
flagrantly advertise, especially in nursing home journals,
drugs to make the patient more manageable, less demanding,
and more tranquil. Staffs demand these and physicians
acquiese, often masking symptoms of treatable illness as
well as creating the potential for permanent irreparable
harm. Further, reaction to chemotherapy can be very
different in the old from that in the young, a fact to
which little attention is given and about which little
is known by most medical practitioners.[43]

A final evidence of the low regard for the aged by
health professionals is the misuse of elderly patients
in research and training, not unlike the violations documented for institutionalized mentally retarded, psychiatric patients and prisoners. "Informed consent" is too
often neither informed nor consenting. This includes
not only drugs, but even goes so far as to encompass
drastic surgical procedures, even grossly disfiguring
surgery, without valid assumption of benefit to the
patient, but which medical students need to learn. Anyone associated with a medical teaching institution is
aware of the practice.[44]

Insofar as maintaining health and preventing illness
are concerned, the promulgation of geriatric health centers for routine health surveillance has not yet been
incorporated into either governmental or private health
planning considerations. Were such facilities available
and staffed by personnel trained in gerontology and
geriatric patient care, it is not only possible, but
highly probable that there would be less need for in-
patient treatment of the more seriously ill. It is also
likely that mental changes related to physical illness
and disease would be identified and treated holistically.
From a purely financial standpoint, healthier people

73

require fewer services from others, including from official agencies.

Mental Health. With regard to the special area of mental illness, documented extent of need for professional care is based upon limited surveys and value judgments. Furthermore, the various studies and surveys have not used common diagnostic criteria for identifying what was judged to be mental illness. Less than one per cent of persons over 65 years of age in the United States are patients in psychiatric hospitals, including both public and private facilities.[45] It is also known that this population is a combination of those who have suffered brain changes in later life, those who have been hospitalized for long periods and have grown old suffering psychotic disorders, and, of course, some are persons who should never have been there at all. The nursing home population also includes a substantial number of persons, estimated to be 50 per cent, who have serious psychiatric problems. This total number of older persons with psychiatric disorders who are in institutions, however, is largely comprised of the oldest segment of the elderly population, and represents perhaps no more than 3 per cent of all those who are 65 years and over.[46]

In contrast, reports of studies made for samples of non-institutionalized elderly give results that range from approximately 12 to 35 per cent of older persons who have mental disabilities judged to range from severe to mild. A more commonly used prevalance estimate is 15 per cent.[47] Adding confusion to this issue and affecting confidence in the estimates reported are several considerations not adequately treated. Among these are: (1) If a person is actually functioning in the community, does he have a severe psychiatric problem? (2) How many of those who have become mentally ill in later life have age related organic brain change problems and how many have personality problems that developed in younger years which have become accentuated in old age? (3) How many are demonstrating stress reactions to environmental conditions and changes, to catastrophe and grief that may not be permanent were stress relieved? (4) How many have physical conditions, chemotherapies, or mineral and/or vitamin deficiencies that affect either personality or mental competence, or both? And, (5) a final intriguing question in view of common stereotypes about the old, is whether the eccentric behavior of the young is translated into psychotic behavior when they are old. Without these answers, any assumption of gross age related change could

74

be fallacious.

Regardless of the extent of the problem, the availability of therapeutic care is minimal. For the most part, psychiatrists, psychologists, therapists and others in mental health professions are neither qualified for nor actually interested in evaluating and treating elderly patients with mental health needs either as inpatients or out-patients.[48] Further, older persons are reluctant to seek their help. Government health care programs offer limited service in this area of disability. Medicare severely limits its coverage for psychiatric services, and Medicaid patients are being shifted from public hospitals to other facilities ill equipped to handle mental illness, such as nursing homes and homes for the aged.

Yet another example of beneficence gone astray is the Federally initiated and state implemented program of deinstitutionalization. The goal here was to get long term elderly patients out of state and local mental hospitals where some had lived for 20, 30, or more years. Between 1969 and 1973, the population of elderly persons in these hospitals decreased 40 per cent.[49] The cry was that they should never have been put there, but had been dumped by families and had become wards of the state. This, in fact, is true for many. But, in old age, these institutions, with all of their faults and inadequacies, had become home, and they afforded the security of the familiar. Suddenly, hordes of these frail elderly were uprooted to nursing homes, old age homes, lonely rooms on back streets in unfamiliar towns, or worse. In the American tradition of seeking instant and immediate solutions for complex problems, and given the nation's propensity for catch phrases, slogans and labels, "deinstitutionalization" was embraced enthusiastically and executed with little or no preparation. Confused, bewildered, and often sick old people were "reinstitutionalized" in unfamiliar and uncaring facilities, transferred to the financial responsibility of the Federal government, and states were relieved of their cost.[50] This is one more case of governmental policy, regluation and precipitancy affecting the health and welfare of the aged that has demonstrated a woeful lack of humanitarianism.

Insofar as government programs are concerned, keeping people alive at all costs has been given primacy, while attention to a happy, healthy life prolonged has been secondary. Even the terminally ill have been denied pain killing relief through the perpetuation of archaic

75

drug control laws that deny extenuating circumstances.
The young drug addict is given more supportive treatment during withdrawal from use of illegal drugs than
is the irrevocably ill old person wracked by unconsion-
able agony as he dies a slow death, too often artificially prolonged.

In summary, despite the multi-billion dollar cost
of Federal health programs in effect for elderly persons,
the provisions available are distinguished by their inadequacies. First, the major need of all older persons
is for comprehensive health maintenance, and this has
not yet received attention at either the policy making
or service delivery levels. Second, many elderly persons could purchase their health maintenance, aided by
public and private insurance plans, but the health professions have largely ignored the need to train practitioners in geriatric patient care or even in understanding the aging process. As a result, competent and skilled health surveillance for the aged is seldom available
for purchase at any price. Third, the Medicare program,
constructed specifically for elderly people, demonstrates
a fundamental ignorance of primary health needs of older
persons. The emphasis is upon hospitalization for acute
illness, which disregards the fact that the elderly have
fewer acute illnesses and more chronic conditions. The
latter require such scantily provided services as home
care and rehabilitative therapies, or others that are
entirely omitted, such as, vision, hearing and dental
protheses, foot care, and out-patient prescription drugs.
Fourth, the costs to the individual over that covered by
Medicare insurance has continued to escalate as the result of increased premiums and deductable portions of
health care costs which the aged individual must pay.
Finally, the unwillingness of many physicians and other
health professionals to accept elderly patients reflects
not only their feelings of inadequacy but also the low
esteem in which aging and the aged are held in the health
industry. In some instances when physicians call themselves geriatric specialists and thereby capitalize on
the demand, investigation reveals they have no training
in the field and their specialized credentials are self-
awarded. Health maintenance and effective treatment in
times of illness are major components for the good life
during the later years, and these have not yet been given
either realistic consideration or practical implementation for older Americans.

A Place to Live

There are few words in the English language more emotionally charged than is the word "home". Through generations of social change and reassignment of values, a persistent goal has been a "home of my own". It represents the conviviality of togetherness, but also the essence of privacy and security. The older one becomes, usually the more committed he is to maintaining that small space in which he can control his life amid the familiar and the comfortable reminders of years past.[51] If he changes location, he carried with him the continuity of his life in his possessions, and he opens and shuts his door to the outside world at will. Home is a concept as well as a place.

In today's manipulated environment of the elderly, they have shown strongest resistance to leaving their old homes, regardless of conditions and circumstances. Their fierce determination to stay in place is not entirely controlled by the building itself, but more by the threat to their independence, life style and memories that may be violated.[52] With such high-flown labels as "alternatives to institutionalization," "living arrangements" and "congregate living," the bureaucracy has dehumanized that warm and wonderful word "home". In the private sector, the need to have choices is largely ignored.

Actually there are few alternatives available to elderly persons in most communities. Since the sixties, there has been an upsurge in Federally financed housing for the aged under the unappealing label of "senior housing". In the main, this is located in larger cities and is comprised of tall apartment buildings located in what are characterized as "high density areas of the aged poor". Eligibility for occupancy is related to assets and income levels as well as age, and space allocations for each unit are not generous. In some of the buildings, built-in furniture has imposed strict controls on how many possessions a tenant may bring with him. Although the safety of these facilities is emphasized with provision of building security controls, call systems, hall railing, grab bars in bathrooms, a resident manager to serve as the tenant advocate, it is still possible for an old person to die in his apartment and his death go undetected for days. Some elderly persons have found happiness in the safety and modern facilities of these buildings, and have accepted the conditions of invasive personal disclosures of means tests. For those who moved from high crime areas, the freedom from fear in the secure buildings is a priority consideration. Others, however, reject not only the "welfare" connotation, but the restricted and custodial age segregated environment as well.

Since the Nation's elderly come from many cultural backgrounds and life styles, even within a single state, how they will want to spend their later years must be related to how they have lived in previous years. Relatively few persons now old have lived in small stacked compartments high above the streets and the normal flow of people. A second factor related to lifestyle is that, for persons now living, the chances of ever requiring institutional care are small. Implicit in this fact is that a majority of elderly people will be able to maintain their own way of life as they wish to live it into very old age or for life. If the capability for prolonged independence is a reality, as is claimed, this too must be incorporated into considerations of what are the feasible choices among suitable homes when the big house, the yard and the stairs become too much to manage.

Despite the relative normalcy of having a choice about where one lives, the scope of alternative living possibilities in later life continues to be extremely narrow. Living in the home of other family members, a home for the aged, "senior housing" or a nursing home are the only four alternatives generally available. The fourth named, a nursing home, should be totally unacceptable as a "housing" choice since it is not a normal mode of living, but belongs in the continuum of health care institutions, not of homes. For the individual whose health has deteriorated to where treatment and nursing care are essential, or whose disease or disability is life threatening without constant monitoring and the availability of emergency services, a nursing home may be needed. Or, for the convalescent patient who needs therapies but not hospitalization, a nursing home may be the health care provision that is required for a limited time. Except when one of these conditions exists, there is no reason on earth to justify "living" even briefly in the abnormal setting of a health care institution. This reduces the alternatives for housing to three more commonly offered throughout the United States.

Another consideration that clouds the issue of what constitutes viable alternatives for a home in later life

is the chronological age criterion superimposed upon
eligibility requirements. For age segregated housing,
this requirement may range from the early fifties to
sixty-five years as a prerequisite for the contracting
tenant. Such a criterion combines with the limited
availability of housing choices to encourage some
individuals to make application prior to or immediately
upon retirement, when they are well, strong and have no
particular need for the proffered services. The result
is that some could spend 30 to 35 years in a supportive
environment, thinking of themselves as old, while only
a relative few will have need of such modified housing
until they are much older. Far more realistic is the
concept of late old age, from 75 years on, as the period
when some elderly persons will function better in a less
demanding and more protected environment. As modern
knowledge pushes healthy old age to increasingly later
chronological age, society, led by a bureaucracy for the
aging, hastens its onset to begin in what are today the
middle years.

   Private Housing Facilities for the Elderly. It is
in the private sector that early age eligibility for
housing is most pronounced, particularly in the old age
communities and in specially constructed apartments and
condominiums. Churches and religious organizations have
tended to go the route of homes for the aged and retirement complexes with all of the private housing targeted
toward the more financially secure elderly. If the property is not an outright purchase, residents usually
pay rather large entrance fees and substantial monthly
charges.* In church sponsored facilities there is usually
a guarantee of care for life. The financial arrangement
most often is irrevocable by the resident after six to
12 months without loss of the initial investment. On the
other hand, there is no assurance that the corporate
management cannot default on the agreement, and then the
resident investor may lose all of his initial investment.
Such has happened.[53]

   Although these protected environments do afford
safety, security and freedom from many chores while pre-
serving varying degrees of freedom of movement, they also

_____

   * In the church sponsored homes for the aged, it is a common
practice to offer a few "scholarships" to cover the initial entrance
payment for poorer members of that religious faith. The number is
limited for each institution and covers the lowest priced units
only.

·relieve the residents of many of the responsibilities and choices normally available to the average adult. A key point which seems to have been largely ignored in the process of managing and manipulating older persons under the guise of protecting them is that stress is an essential ingredient in a healthy life. Without stress, there is no challenge, and without challenge living is degraded to existing, encouraging both mental and physical deterioration. Admittedly, when stress is elevated to unrelieved frustration, the results are negative, but stress within normal tolerance limits is the essential basis for achievement throughout all of life.[54]

Despite the limitations apparent in the planned housing and communities for older citizens, even more dangerous are the unplanned migrations of old people to some of the sun-belt areas where they congregate in enclaves. There, on the outskirts of the community's activities, they sometimes find life less than fulfilling while inflated costs deny many even basic necessities on incomes no longer minimally adequate. Their independence then becomes a trap, and their mounting needs go unrecognized or ignored and unmet.[55]

Although prevalence of other types of choices for a place to live is rather sketchy, there are older people who have found some of the normal alternatives available to other age groups. One in limited supply is the new community development, such as the Leisure Worlds, located primarily in the West and Southwest. Here people live as they wish in condominiums designed for an older population. Many services and facilities are available, some routine and others upon request, but their use is determined by the residents, and security provisions are comprehensive. The purchase cost is moderate and the monthly charges, including principal, interest, insurance, maintenance, taxes, gardening, recreational facilities, minibuses and management, are not only reasonable but, in some instances, not greater than charges made in public housing considering the differences in extent of services.

A modification of the community concept is the mobile home park which caters to older persons. Some of these are quite elaborate, while others are much less plush. Still other elderly persons have found more congenial those parks that serve diverse ages, where they live with neighbors both younger and older than themselves.

In cities with large apartment complexes, there has been a growing trend toward renting certain specified units or buildings to persons with children and other buildings to those without children. In the latter there is a wide age range of tenants, and the young and the old seem to find one another compatible.

Some elderly persons also have found solutions in hotels, rooms and apartments, boarding homes, in renovated older buildings converted to housing, and in remodeled houses providing two or more apartments with some maintenance responsibilities assumed by the tenants. These arrangements include those that are less than desirable, but others of the same type are both comfortable and convenient. The problem lies not in the nature of the alternatives, but in the quality of the facilities, their locations, and the limitations imposed by the extent of supply and demand.

Federal Housing. More highly visible is government financed and operated public housing, which usually is designated as "subsidized housing for the poor". Interestingly enough, that constructed for the elderly has a designated eligibility commonly described and officially labeled as "for persons with low incomes who are 65 years of age, blind or handicapped." Here again, there is policy reinforcement of old as being one of the major disabilities, and those who are old having common needs with others in the disabled population, although many in the latter group also are independent and self-sufficient.

Federal public housing programs for the elderly and those for the general population of eligible persons, including the elderly, are distinguished by the complexities, inequities and confusion. Since the sixties, the government has been increasingly involved in housing for the aged poor, with separate and distinct programs in effect under the Departments of Housing and Urban Development, the Federal Housing Administration and the Department of Agriculture. Under the various uncoordinated legislative acts, there are low rent housing; rent supplements; direct long term, low interest loans for construction; mortgage insurance; purchase and rehabilitation of properties by housing authorities for "leased housing"; as well as low interest rehabilitation loans and grants for low income home owners. These do not include the housing component of the Model Cities Program, other housing improvement alternatives, or nursing home construction funding, which also comprise provisions under the the various legislative acts.[56]

Since there is no planning base for all of these

81

government programs, location of the facilities has a
happenstance relationship to need, with some communities having a great deal and others none at all. Additionally, the diffusion of programs, all with different
regulations and qualification requirements, presents
problems for their use. Among the "rules" hazards is
one condition in which public housing eligibility is so
rigidly established that persons may be too poor to
qualify.[57] An interesting phenomenon.

Still another component of the housing confusion is
the urban renewal program, also financed by the Federal
government. Under this, thousands of elderly persons in
central cities have been evicted and their homes destroy-
ed without prior preparation for housing those displac-
ed.[58]

On the subject of government support of housing
problems for the aged, one dramatic example is that of
old, often hazardous hotels in large inner cities where
low income elderly persons congregate. Supported by
Federal monies for minimal services, many old people,
including the frail and the sick, exist in the confines
of their rooms and the lobbies, fearful of crime ridden
streets and of their own limitations for coping with
their ghetto environment. In these old buildings, long
discarded by the public at large, the elderly give mute
evidence of government support of the problem rather than
action to solve it.

Tangential to government housing programs are others,
primarily under the sponsorship of the Federal Administration on Aging and Title XX of the Social Security Act,
which offer a proliferation of support services in the
home. For the qualifying poor, there are home repair
services, winterization programs, home security assistance, companion and chore services, homemaker and home
health aides, and others. These provide spotty custodial
type help to those who qualify, who seek it out, and who
document their poverty.

Summary. All of these fragmented housing programs
neither solve the problems nor offer any coordinated
practical approach to solution. The cost is in the
billions while the benefits are minimal to the population
of older persons in the United States as a whole. Neither
private enterprise nor the Federal government has truly
faced the nature of the need and its growing impact. In
a message to Congress in 1973, the President estimated
that the government had expended approximately 90 billion

dollars for public and subsidized housing since 1937.
He reported that one government study had concluded that
it costs between 15 and 40 per cent more for the government to provide housing than it would cost were the same
housing acquired by people from the private market.[59]
Whether or not this report would be supported to the
extent cited in further investigation, there is reason
to believe that the uncoordinated hodgepodge of legislative acts with their extensive bureaucratic conditions,
controls and conflicting regulations is more expensive
than effective. The solution lies in alternatives among
which individual elderly people can make free choices.
At this time and for all practical purposes, the housing
choices in a majority of communities throughout the
nation continue to be completely independent, isolated
living or an essentially custodial or protective type
facility. Almost no cognizance has been taken of the
safe, convenient and diverse alternative home environments between the two. It is, however, in this vacuum
between the extremes that a preponderance of the escalating housing needs of the elderly lies, and it is in the
diversity of communities throughout the nation that the
solutions can and should be sought and found.

The Federal government continues to award grants and
contracts for researchers to study the elderly and their
environments, their attitudes toward home, to public
housing and their adjustments or lack of same, their
socialization patterns, et cetera. All of this investigation may have become counterproductive, impeding and
delaying rather than aiding problem solutions. The time
has come for action, not further reflection. The old are
getting older, and they do not have time to wait. Positive steps can be taken using knowledge and resources
already available.

Something to Do

The majority of elderly persons are active and involved with family, community, paid and volunteer work,
and as caretakers of their own affairs. They also are
not lonely, are seldom bored, and they are not socially
isolated.* Further, they are a highly heterogeneous population, as they were when they were young. Actually,
evidence supports the fact that people grow increasingly
less alike as they age and are actually more heterogeneous in old age than they were earlier in life.[60]

* See Chapter II.

Despite all the evidence to the contrary, Federal programs have been constructed and funded with ever increasing generosity to combat assigned common problems of the aged, namely, loneliness, isolation, boredom and inactivity. As appropriations have increased steadily, there has been mushrooming growth throughout the country of programs to solve these "problems", such as, recreation for the aged, instructional courses, senior centers, parties, craft programs, meals for the aged, games, trips, and a host of others. Like children, they are organized and shepherded through their activities under the leadership usually of bright and cheerful young people committed to improving the lives of these "poor old people".

These programs only serve to reinforce the growing practice of benign manipulation of elderly adults, telling them when, where and what to eat, what games to play, where to shop, how to travel. This may be simply an expensive depreciation of the aged, supporting the old myths of their inadequacy and inability. In fact, such negative views of the old previously were a part of the cultural heritage supported only by the viability of man's stereotyped thinking; now they are legislated and enhanced by what is fast becoming a National policy of "ageism". Afforded the opportunity to live comfortably, safely and with adequate income for life's necessities, old people may effectively demonstrate that their sixty, seventy or eighty years of managing their own affairs have equipped them eminently well to function as independent, dignified, elderly adults still managing their lives.

How often one hears the protest from older persons, "Why do they want me to play games, when what I need is someone to repair my screen door? I am perfectly capable of entertaining myself." Or, "I don't want someone to give me a meal. Why don't they bring prices down so I can afford what I need?" These are valid questions to which honest answers are in order.

According to the Harris Survey, there still is a strong interest in work and employment among the over 65 age population. While only 12 per cent are employed, another 6 per cent are actively seeking work, or a total of 18 per cent who must be considered an integral part of the labor force. And, this is only the tip of the iceberg of the employment problem for older Americans. Some 37 per cent of retired workers said they were retired involuntarily, and did not want to stop working. This all adds up to a substantial proportion of workers 65 years

of age and older who are employed or would like to be
wage earners.[61]

   In addition, 22 per cent of the elderly are engaged
in unpaid volunteer work, with another 10 per cent who
wished to do this, but had not yet found acceptance.
Some of those doing volunteer work also are employed.[62]

   Previously, the question was raised concerning the
relative few who participate in segregated government
nutrition/socialization programs. Louis Harris seems to
give a part of the answer when he reports that 74 per
cent of older persons say that "they would prefer to
spend most of their time with people not of their own
age, but with people of all ages." The following are
some of the things they said they were doing:

   34% run errands for their children and grandchildren;
   39% give advice on how to deal with life's problems;
   45% help out by actually giving their younger kin money;
   54% take care of small children in the family;
   68% help out when someone is ill, and
   90% help their offspring by giving them gifts.[63]

Were the issue of something to do, of loneliness and
isolation treated realistically, it would appear that
this is a problem of manageable proportions for the few,
with solution within each community and its agencies and
services, without a separate bureaucracy to manage it.

   The truth is that bureaucratic publicity reinforces
public perception of the aged as incompetent, frail, sad,
lonely and, in fact, inferior citizens to be protected,
entertained and "wet-nursed" through their second childhood. Nothing could be more fallacious. Illustrative
examples of the difference between public perception of
problems related to the old and views of the elderly
themselves are:[64]

Problems Among Older Persons	Perception of Extent of Problems:	
	Persons Under 65 Years Old	Persons Over 65 Years Old
Suffer loneliness	61%	12%
Feel unneeded	56%	7%
Do not have enough to eat	38%	6%
Have too few friends	28%	5%

There is little doubt that the percentages of the elderly who have these problems can be matched by equal or greater percentages among younger age populations. As a case in point, according to a University of Nebraska study[65] to determine the loneliest people in the United States, the rank order reported was:

1. college students
2. divorced people
3. welfare recipients
4. single mothers
5. rural students
6. housewives
7. the elderly

Here the aged were able to achieve only seventh place, a not very impressive rank in the order of most lonely components of the total population. Were the old returned their citizenship rights to full participation in the marketplace, in the community and in all aspects of social action, they no doubt would rank even lower in prevalence of loneliness.

While a younger population is learning how to do many things as well as exploring what they want to do, the old already know what they can do and how to do it, what they want to learn and, usually, where they can learn it. They also know the difference between solitude and loneliness, and savor the former as a part of life.

Mr. Harris sums up the problem succinctly when he states that the basic libel about treatment of the elderly "is that they are not allowed to contribute their skills, their energies, their drive, which has (sic) simply not left most of them. The basic libel is that people are declared dead and useless before their time."[66]

For the majority, they do not need nor want something contrived for them to do, but rather they want to do what they do best; they do not want to be entertained, but to entertain themselves; not to be served, but to serve. There is no need for an agency to interpret the elderly or their needs for they give strong evidence that they can speak for themselves. Their problem is one of closed doors. Once age segregation barriers to employment, community and the full gamut of normal citizen activity and responsibility are removed, the majority of the old will walk unassisted into all of the diversities of a full life.

The Constraints of Service: A Summary

It becomes evident, even in a brief survey of some of the more publicized Federal programs, that the legislated provisions for older Americans are seriously flawed in both their conceptualization and in their delivery. Beginning with the title of the bill, the Older Americans Act, there is implicit a universality of applicability with all older Americans included simply because none is excluded. This, however, is far from being the case.

The conditions and provisions built into the Act and into the implementing regulations are largely restrictive, limiting major benefits to the Federally defined poor. The result is that only a minority of elderly persons are included. In 1975, Dr. Herman Brotman reported that 15.3 per cent of the over 65 aged population had incomes below the official Federal poverty level, in contrast with the 21.6 per cent so categorized in 1971. When the 1975 "near poor" were added, the segment of the older population included rose to 25.4 per cent, in contrast with the 32 per cent in 1971. During the same period, families at the poverty level declined from 14.2 per cent to 8 per cent, while the financial status for individuals dropped from 42.3 per cent to 31 per cent. This means that during a four-year period a rather dramatic improvement had occurred. Based upon these data, the only conclusion to be drawn is that a majority of older Americans have incomes substantially above the Federally established poverty level. Admittedly, there is much reason to question the Federally defined demarcation line that separates "poverty" from "near poverty" in the face of the economic realities of today's world.

As one final irony in the farcical construction of the government "benefit" programs is the condition which prescribes that a person at the Federally defined poverty level may be too "rich" to obtain benefits. If he receives $120.00 a month from earned Social Security covered employment but a lifetime of saving for emergencies has produced a savings account of $3,000, then he is ineligible for food stamps or for an income supplement until he has dissipated half of that savings account. It must be reduced to $1,500 before he can obtain the pittance of supplementary help. In contrast, a person who has never worked and never saved may have all of the benefits without question. It is a harsh benefactor who penalizes frugality and self-help.

Limiting attention only to the approximately 25 per cent called "poor" and "near poor," even here there are fundamental constraints for obtaining benefits. By the very nature of the intrusiveness of requirements for qualifying for assistance, the elderly poor suffer the embarrassment of a public declaration of their poverty. For this reason, some of these old people have rejected the old age assistance programs, preferring to retain their pride and dignity as too important to be compromised. Official sympathy for the aged has not extended to acknowledgement of how they feel about themselves nor to respect for the values by which they live.

Pursuing further the matter of income and the financial status of elderly Americans, the history of the Social Security fund is a prime example of legislators' capricious actions in changing it from its intended purpose. As conceived and sold, it was an insurance program for workers to supplement their savings and the then few other pension programs. The initial planners estimated that, with an increased tax rate of six per cent by 1949, the Social Security program would be self-sufficient up to 1980 at least, and would have accumulated a trust reserve approaching 50 billion dollars. The emphasis was upon individual worker equity with workers both the contributors and the beneficiaries from their own labors. But, immediately after passage of the Act and continuing for over 40 years since, the erosion of this concept has grown. At this point, it is possible for a single person to have paid the maximum tax throughout his or her long working career and to receive nothing should he die before retirement. In contrast, a young married worker who has paid almost nothing and dies may leave beneficiaries who will eventually receive hundreds of thousands of dollars in benefits. Yet, upon retirement, the two workers will receive the same, plus all of the added benefits for the beneficiaries of the worker with dependents. In short, the worker benefit program has long been abandoned, while the social welfare aspects of the system have been over-extended to the point that individual worker-retirees are the least benefited, as demonstrated by the percentage of individual worker beneficiaries whose savings in Social Security produce poverty and near poverty incomes. In reality, the elderly have contributed a growing percentage of their wages to a Federal pension plan only to become recipients in a Federal welfare program when they retire. And, the dependency role of the elderly does not stop here.

The importance that old people attach to health,

home and adequate income has not been matched in priorities assigned to their needs by government. Instead,
proposals made and programs developed in these areas
have concentrated upon maintaining the problems rather
than solving them. This insures perpetuation of the administrative structure, but does little to change the
life circumstances that need to be changed. The result
is that the aged toward whom the programs are directed
more and more occupy an imposed dependency role, with
the proclaimed need becoming a self-fulfilling prophecy.
The only problem with this, aside from the tremendous
financial cost, is that the aged who were targeted for
benefit become the victims of the rigid constraints.

Over and over throughout this Nation's history it
has been demonstrated that life styles and life satisfactions cannot be mandated. Evidence is cumulative
that the "melting pot" of America is a diverse and dis-
similar society held together by a common belief in the
right to be different, to walk out-of-step. These are
the old Americans, but also the young. Because of their
very heterogeneity these old people are ill equipped to
combat the mounting and stultifying constraints being
imposed upon them by the awesome powers of government.

Although the voices of lobbyists are strong and
those who lobby highly visible as they clamor for ever
greater regulation over the lives of older citizens, the
majority of elderly Americans still want independence.
They want those things that make independence possible -
available health maintenance, an equitable living income,
choices freely exercised, and the respect rightfully
theirs. What they do not want is charity, limits, superimposed complexities or depreciation. In short, they
appear very much like all of their fellow citizens of
younger years.

FOOTNOTES AND REFERENCES

Footnotes

1

Robert C. Atchley. The Social Forces in Later Life. (Second Edition). Wadsworth Publishing Company. Belmont, California. 1977. p. 259.

2

"Speaker Attacks Stereotyped and Outmoded Views About Filial Responsibilities to Aged." Geriatric Focus. Vol. 9, No. 3. March 1970. pp. 2 and 6, and Margaret Hellie Huyck. Growing Older, Chapter 5. "Parents and Children: Showdown at Generation Gap." Prentice-Hall, Inc. Englewood Cliffs, New Jersey. 1974. pp. 69-85.

3

Jon Hendricks and C. Davis Hendricks. Aging in Mass Society: Myths and Realities. Winthrop Publishers, Inc. Cambridge, Massachusetts. 1977. p. 329.

4

Toward a National Policy on Aging, Vol. I. Proceedings of the 1971 White House Conference on Aging. Washington, D. C. 1973. p. 3, and Thomas H. McGavack. "Notes on the Second White House Conference on Aging." The Journal of the American Geriatrics Society, Vol. XX, No. 5. p. 194.

5

Toward a National Policy on Aging, Vol. I. op. cit. p. 3.

6

The Older Americans Act of 1965.

7

Ibid.

8

Ibid.

9

Yung Ping Chen. Income. Background Paper for 1971 White House Conference on Aging. Administration on Aging. Washington, D. C. 1970, and

U. S. Senate Special Committee on Aging. Economics
of Aging: Toward a Full Share in Abundance. U. S.
Government Printing Office. Washington, D. C. 1970.

10

Toward a National Policy on Aging, Vols. I and II.
Op. cit.

11

The Post-White House Conference on Aging Reports, 1973.
Sub-Committee on Aging of Committee on Labor and
Public Welfare and Special Committee on Aging, U. S.
Senate. U. S. Government Printing Office. Washing-
ton, D. C. 1973.

12

Marian L. MacDonald. "The Forgotten Americans: A
Sociopsychological Analysis of Aging and Nursing
Homes." American Journal of Community Psychology.
Vol. I, No. 3. 1973.

13

Thomas H. McGavack. Op. cit. p. 199.

Role Assignment by Statute

Footnotes

14

The Older Americans Act of 1965 and Comprehensive
Amendments to the Older American's Act, 1973. U. S.
Government Printing Office. Washington, D. C.

15

U. S. Department of Labor, Bureau of Labor Statistics.
Employment and Earnings. Vol. 22, No. 7. January,
1976.

16

James E. Birren, et al. (Editors)   Human Aging. Public
Health Service, National Institute of Mental Health.
U. S. Department of Health, Education and Welfare.
Publication No. (HSM) 71-9051. U. S. Government
Printing Office. Washington, D. C. 1971. pp. 284-
285, 314.

17

Byron Gold, Elizabeth Kutza, and Theodore R. Marmor.
"United States Social Policy on Old Age: Present

Patterns and Predictions." Social Policy, Social
Ethics, and the Aging Society. Bernice L. Neugarten
and Robert J. Havighurst. (Editors)   U. S. Government
Printing Office. Washington, D. C. 1977. pp. 10-15.

Additional References

Butler, Robert N. Why Survive? Being Old in America.
    Harper and Row, Publishers, Inc. New York, New York.
    1975.

Comfort, Alex. A Good Age. Crown Publishers, New York,
    New York. 1976.

Heron, Alastair and Sheila Chown. Age and Function.
    Little, Brown & Company. Boston, Massachusetts.
    1967.

Older Americans Act of 1965, As Amended. Administration
    on Aging, Office of Human Development. U. S. Depart-
    ment of Health, Education and Welfare. DHEW Publi-
    cation No. (OHD) 76-20170. March, 1976.

Shock, Nathan W. (Editor)   Prospectives in Experimental
    Gerontology. Charles C. Thomas. Springfield,
    Illinois. 1966.

_____, and A. H. Norris. "Neuromuscular Coord-
    ination as a Factor in Age Changes in Muscular Exer-
    cise." Physical Activity and Aging. D. Brunner and
    E. Jokl. (Editors)   S. Karger. New York, New York.
    1970.

Strehler, Bernard L. Time, Cells, and Aging. Academic
    Press. New York, New York. 1962.

Rediscovery of the Dole

Social Security

Footnotes

18

    Donald G. Fowles. Income and Poverty Among the Elderly,
    1975. Statistical Reports on Older Americans. U. S.
    Department of Health, Education and Welfare. Wash-
    ington, D. C. April, 1977. Table 3.

19
  Ibid. Table D, p. 6.

20
  Herman B. Brotman. "Tncome and Poverty in the Older
    Population in 1978." The Gerontologist, Vol. 17,
    No. 1. 1977. pp. 24-25.

21
  "The Elderly in America." Population Bulletin, Vol. 30,
    No. 3. Population Reference Bureau, Inc. Washington,
    D. C. 1975. p. 15.

Additional References

Boskin, Michael J. (Editor) The Crisis in Social
    Security: Problems and Prospects. Institute for
    Contemporary Studies. San Francisco, California.
    1977. pp. 1-40.

Characteristics of the Population Below the Poverty Level.
    Current Population Reports. Series P-60, No. 106.
    U. S. Government Printing Office. Washington, D. C.
    1977.

Demographic and Economic Characteristics of the Aged, 1968.
    Social Security Survey. Social Security Administra-
    tion, Office of Research and Statistics. U. S. De-
    partment of Health, Education and Welfare. Research
    Report No. 45. DHEW Publication No. (SSA) 75-11802.
    U. S. Government Printing Office. Washington, D. C.
    1975.

Hudson, Robert B. "The 'Graying' of the Federal Budget
    and Its Consequences for Old-Age Policy." The
    Gerontologist, Vol. 18, No. 5 (Part I). October,
    1978. pp. 428-440.

Murrell, Alicia H. The Future of Social Security. The
    Brookings Institution. Washington, D. C. 1977.
    pp. 1-24.

Social Security: The First Thirty-Five Years. Occasional
    Papers in Gerontology, No. 7. Institute on Gerontol-
    ogy. The University of Michigan-Wayne State Univer-
    sity. Ann Arbor, Michigan. 1970. pp. 1-60.

Footnotes

22
    The Older Americans Act of 1965, Amendments, 1972,
    Title VII - Nutrition Program for the Elderly, and
    subsequent amendments through 1978.

23
    Federal Register, Part II, August 19, 1972 and Part III,
    November 15, 1977. Superintendent of Documents,
    U. S. Government Printing Office. Washington, D. C.

24
    The Myth and Reality of Aging in America. Louis Harris
    and Associates, Inc. The National Council on the
    Aging. Washington, D. C. 1976. pp. 141-142.

25
    "Nutrition Topic of NVOILA." Perspective on Aging,
    Vol. VII, No. 6. November/December, 1978. National
    Council on the Aging. Washington, D. C. p. 18.

26
    The Proposed Fiscal 1976 Budget: What It Means for Older
    Americans. Staff Report. Senate Special Committee
    on Aging, U. S. Congress. 1975. p. 1.

27
    Authorizations for 1976 and 1977 appropriations were
    added to Older Americans Act by the 1974 Amendments,
    and for fiscal year 1978 by the 1975 Amendments.

28
    Comprehensive Older Americans Act Amendments of 1978.
    U. S. House of Representatives, Conference Report,
    Ninety-Fifth Congress, Report No. 95-1618.
    September 22, 1978. p. 5.

29
    Valinda Jones. "House, Senate Settles Differences to
    Reauthorizing OAA for Three Years." Perspective
    on Aging, Vol. VII, No. 5. 1978. p. 22.

30
    Older Americans Act of 1965, As Amended. Published
    March, 1976 (Bicentenial Compilation). National
    Council on the Aging. Washington, D. C. p. 57.

Means Tests

Footnotes

31
The Interrelationships of Benefit Programs for the
Elderly. Federal Council on the Aging. Washington,
D. C. 1975.

32
Ibid.

33
Title XX of the Social Security Act: A Resource for
Serving the Needs of Older People. National Council
on the Aging. Washington, D. C. 1976.

Additional References

Handbook of Federal Programs Benefitting Older Americans.
Federal Council on the Aging. Washington, D. C.
1975.

Paperwork and the Older Americans Act: Problems of Implementing Accountability. Staff Information Paper prepared for the U. S. Senate Special Committee on Aging.
U. S. Government Printing Office. Washington, D. C.
1978.

In Sickness and in Health

Footnotes

34
Robert N. Butler. "Medicine and Aging: An Assessment of
Opportunities and Neglect." Testimony before the
U. S. Senate, Special Committee on Aging. October
13, 1976. National Institute on Aging. Public
Health Service, U. S. Department of Health, Educa-
tion and Welfare. Bethesda, Maryland.

35
Ibid.

36
Robin M. Henig. "Exposing the Myth of Senility." New
York Times. December 3, 1978.

·37
    Peter M. Berdy. "Letter to the Editor." The Gerontol-
    ogist, Vol. 13, No. 3, Part I. 1973. The Geronto-
    logical Society. Washington, D. C. p. 275.

38
    Robert N. Butler. op. cit., and
    Raymond Harris. "Geriatrics American Style." Perspec-
    tive on Aging, Vol. VIII, No. 1. 1979. pp. 13-15.

39
    Robert N. Butler. Why Survive? Being Old In America.
    Harper & Row, Publishers, Inc. New York, New York.
    1975. pp. 18, 204, 231.

40
    Donald C. Spence, et al. "Medical Student Attitudes
    Toward the Geriatric Patient." Journal of the
    American Geriatric Society. Vol. 16: 976-983. New
    York, New York. 1968.

41
    Robert N. Butler. Address before the National Confer-
    ence on County Resource Development for Aging
    Citizens. Shoreham Americana Hotel, Washington,
    D. C. January 10, 1977.

42
    The American Association of Homes for the Aging:
    Washington Report. The Association. Washington,
    D. C. June 26, 1975.

43
    Robert N. Butler. Why Survive? Being Old in America.
    op. cit. pp. 197-201, and
    Robin M. Henig. op. cit.

44
    Butler. Ibid. pp. 201-202, and
    Warren T. Reich. "Ethical Issues Related to Research
    Involving Elderly Subjects." The Gerontologist,
    Vol. 18, No. 4. The Gerontological Society.
    Washington, D. C. 1978. pp. 326-337.

45
    Alexander Simon. Background Paper on Mental Health.
    White House Conference on Aging. Washington, D. C.
    1971.

46
Ewald W. Busse and Eric Pfeiffer. (Editors) Behavior
and Adaptation in Late Life. Little, Brown and
Company. Boston, Massachusetts. 1969. pp. 190-191.

47
Ibid. pp. 190-194.

48
Robert N. Butler. Why Survive? Being Old in America.
op. cit. pp. 231-234.

49
Ibid. p. 24, and
Wilma T. Donahue. "What About Our Responsibility
Toward the Abandoned Elderly?" The Gerontologist,
Vol. 18, No. 2. 1978. p. 105.

50
Donahue. Ibid. pp. 102-111, and
Returning the Mentally Disabled to the Community: Gov-
ernment Needs to do More. Report prepared by U. S.
General Accounting Office. (No. HRD-76-152). OAO
Distribution Section, P. O. Box 1020, Washington,
D. C. January 7, 1977.

Additional References

Health Care for Older Americans: The "Alternatives" Issue.
Hearing before the Special Committee on Aging, United
States Senate, Ninety-Fifth Congress, First Session.
Part I, Washington, D. C. May 16, 1977. U. S.
Government Printing Office. Washington, D. C. 1977.

Lesparre, Michael. "An Interview with Robert N. Butler,
M.D., Director, National Institute on Aging."
Hospitals, Vol. 50. November 16, 1976. pp. 50-56,
59.

"Physician's Role in the Care of the Aging, The." Sympos-
ium Proceedings. The Gerontologist, Vol. 10, No. 1,
Part II. Spring, 1970. Total volume.

Smyer, Michael A. and Margaret Gatz. "Aging and Mental
Health." American Psychologist, Vol. 34, No. 3.
March, 1979. pp. 240-246.

A Place to Live

Footnotes

51
James D. Manney, Jr. Aging in American Society.
Institute of Gerontology, University of Michigan-
Wayne State University. Ann Arbor, Michigan. 1975.
p. 162, and
Robert C. Atchley. The Social Forces in Later Life.
Second Edition. Wadsworth Publishing Company, Inc.
Belmont, California. 1977. p. 200.

52
Robert N. Butler. Why Survive? Being Old in America.
Harper & Row, Publishers, Inc. New York, New York.
1975. pp. 103-104.

53
Columbia Broadcasting System. 60 Minutes. "Old, Middle
Class and Broke." Produced by CBS News. April 23,
1978.

54
Hans Selye. The Stress of Life. McGraw-Hill Book
Company. New York, New York. 1956. pp. vii, 299-
304.

55
Donn Pearce. Dying in the Sun. Charterhouse. New
York, New York. 1974.

56
Robert N. Butler. op. cit. pp. 123-130, and
Rosamond Boyd and Charles Oakes. Foundations of Prac-
tical Gerontology. University of South Carolina
Press. Columbia, South Carolina. 1969. pp. 208-
209.

57
Robert N. Butler. op. cit. p. 114.

58
Ibid. p. 128.

59
"Federal Housing Policy." Message by the President,
September 19, 1973. Congressional Record. p. S.16864.

Additional References

Breger, William. "Innovative Housing Design Could Foster
    Independence." Perspective on Aging, Vol. VI, No. 2.
    March/April 1977. pp. 9-11.

Davis, Richard H. (Editor) Housing for the Elderly.
    Ethel Percy Andrus Gerontology Center. University
    of Southern California. Los Angeles, California.
    1973.

Dickman, Irving R. and Miriam Dickman. Where Older
    People Live: Living Arrangements for the Elderly.
    Public Affairs Pamphlet No. 556. Public Affairs
    Committee, Inc. 381 Park Avenue, South. New York,
    New York. 1978.

Gerontologist, The. Vol. 18, No. 2. Section on Housing.
    April, 1978. pp. 121-158.

_____. Vol. 15, No. 1. Section on Living
    Arrangements. February, 1975. pp. 68-91.

Kart, Cary S. and Barbara B. Manard. Aging in America.
    Alfred Publishing Company. Port Washington, New
    York. 1976. pp. 313-394.

Lawton, M. Powell. "The Relative Impact of Congregate
    and Traditional Housing on Elderly Tenants." The
    Gerontologist, Vol. 16, No. 3. 1976. pp. 237-242.

Something to Do

Footnotes

60
    Robert N. Butler. Why Survive? Being Old in America.
    Harper & Row, Publishers, Inc. New York, New York.
    1975. p. 7, and
    Lillian R. Dangott and Richard A. Kalish. A Time to
    Enjoy: The Pleasures of Aging. Prentice-Hall, Inc.
    Englewood Cliffs, New Jersey. 1979. p. 12.

61
    Louis Harris. "Who the Senior Citizens Really Are,"
    (Excerpts from speech to the National Council on
    Aging.) The Altrusan. December, 1974. p. 10.

62

  Ibid.

63

  Ibid. p. 9.

64

  Ibid. p. 8.

65

  Parade. December 10, 1978. p. 23.

66

  Louis Harris. op. cit. p. 10.

Additional Reference

Robinson, John. How Americans Use Time. Praeger Pub-
    lishers. New York, New York. 1977.

IV

INTRACTABLE OBSTACLES:
EXPEDIENCY, BUREAUCRACY, BENEFACTION

Simple words converted into labels and slogans can
and often do take on a contrived meaning, and with it the
power to exercise a pervasive influence over the minds of
men. The subtlety with which this is achieved may assure
acceptance, even when the meaning of the label is obscure
or actually defies intelligent clarification or interpretation. In recent years, the elderly have been prime
targets for this mechanism, with labels ranging from the
humorous to those that have far more serious consequences.

Many old people themselves are uncomfortable with
terms now so prevalent. They do see a certain wry humor
in being called the "young old" or "old young", especially
when the speaker switches from one to the other, demonstrating his own confusion about what he means. The
terms that vie for their disapproval, however, are
"oldsters", "seniors" and "senior citizens". All of these
labels are totally meaningless. No one ever says to what
the senior is senior, and, of course, "oldster" is not in
the dictionary, so can only be freely interpreted. The
one thing all of these terms have in common is that they
are platitudinous and patronizing. Given the simple alternatives of "old", "aged" and "elderly", which clearly
denote that one is well along in years, there is no need
for contrived less clear terms of reference.[1]

There are two basic reasons for coining the new
labels for old people, both reflecting the value system
of the society. First, on an individual level, one

using such terms in order to avoid the word "old" is
demonstrating his own personal rejection of growing old
and his inability to accept aging changes for himself.
It is in essence a denial of his own aging, and his
palliative attempt to play down this unacceptable condition in others. Second, from a societal standpoint
the labeling establishes a social group in which an
entire chronologically defined population is separated
out, apart from the rest of the citizenry. When the
labels are universalized and officially assigned to
people, the next step is to extend that label to things
associated with them, such as, senior centers, senior
housing or honor roll of seniors. The implications
become increasingly more serious in their effects upon
the old as well as the young, for terms then gain the
weight of a philosophical doctrine rooted in the individual avoidance and rejection of being old.

"Society's Burden"

For a number of years there have been two parallel
developments in the Nation with regard to older citizens
that have produced rather curious results. First was
the early warning about the strain on Social Security as
larger numbers of older persons retired. Second has been
been the development of an expanding Federal bureaucracy
devoted primarily to the impoverished and sick old. Like
an umbrella over both has been the conclusion that greater public monies must be expended to avoid impending
catastrophes. Although the situation which has evolved has
had a certain contrived element, the public, including
the elderly, has been faced implicitly with the alternative of more taxes or more human suffering. Given these
choices, to be against proposed solutions is rather like
being against motherhood and for sin.

As is so often true with a crusading legislature,
the needs, as defined, grew in geometric proportion to
the problem. Statistical studies were marshalled to sus-
tain the conslusions. The actual growth in numbers in the
older population is a fact, but the deduction that this
fact is synonymous with an ever increasing army of dependent, infirm and sick older citizens is where the fallacy
lies. There is no biological law that supports the
assumption that being old means being incompetent as an
inevitability. The dependency role for the elderly is
man made, not a natural force.

What has actually evolved in perhaps no more than

two decades is a growing national commitment to "ageism"[2] as policy. The old now have become a part of the Nation's legislated "minority psychology". To the extend that discrimination against those who had reached a ripe old age with visible changes that did not always enhance their physical attractiveness when compared with youth, the devaluing of old age and those grown old has precedence centuries old. The age old myths and stereotypes about aging have continued long and strong. What has happened more recently in the United States, however, is the enactment of pejorative attitudes into law. The fact that discrimination has become benign makes it no less discriminatory. Actually, a national tolerance for the concept of dependency and inadequacy of the aged may be more discriminating because of its stultifying effects upon the independent and totally adequate majority of those chronologically old.[3]

By acts of Congress, encouraged by single issue lobbyists, the country has acquired a policy of separatism based upon race, sex and now age, with further fragmentations into smaller entities emerging. No longer is it one Nation of the whole comprised of many diverse groups giving richness and strength to a united states and to one another. Instead, it is a nation well on its way to making subcultures, and, indeed, differences weapons to be wielded one against the other. At the point this new culture of conflict is accomplished, the citizenry will become not Americans, but Hispanic Americans, black Americans, handicapped Americans, male or female Americans, all competing one against the other. Since the old like the young cut across all of these "minorities", the futility of what is happening can be more damaging to them for they will be divided among all the other minorities. And, since the young will grow old, where will their fragmented identities lie? The natural progression would seem to be further division into old Hispanics, old blacks, old men, old women, et al, where the old then can compete with one another for a place in the political sun. All of this is farcical. The strength of each sub-group lies in the differences maintained while all share equally in the richness of diversity. Sharing equally does not always mean sharing the same things, for children of all cultural backgrounds need schools, while the old need other emphases. And needs are not stagnant, but vary in different periods of a life, and from one individual to another. The common need that all have throughout life is to move in the mainstream without risk of ever being segregated out of it,

103

·regardless of the bounty that might be won by being excluded.

Being apart from society rather than a part of it also is very expensive in monetary costs because each "minority program" must be operated separately. For example, the over-65 age group categorized as living in poverty and "near poverty" now has been reduced to approximately one-fourth of the total older population in that age range. At the same time, however, legislation, appropriations and the development and expansion of agencies and agency services for the aged poor continue to grow. Since more and more monies and people are needed to deliver services and to regulate the delivery, there is much evidence that the legislation has not only perpetrated the level of the problem, but has also magnified it. Constant reference is made to ever greater needs in senior housing, senior centers, the senior nutrition program, senior volunteers, senior companions, senior recreation, senior transportation, and others.

Ancillary to the direct services programs, there have been appropriations for conferences and workshops to discuss the aged, for research to study aging, and for educational institutions to train students in come aspect of aging. Unquestionably, some of these Federally funded activities have potential for benefit to older persons and for the young who will become old. The regulations controlling such grants, however, also have served to elevate costs as well as to direct the expenditure of funds according to Federally assigned priorities, which may or may not be the greatest need in a particular area or institution. Too often the major benefits from these large expenditures of tax monies have been: (1) the prestige of grantsmanship in the receiving program or institution, (2) the personal professional status value to the individual grant recipient, and (3) the anti-poverty value of the jobs created for the staffs employed. Direct positive results for the elderly have been limited. Since the states and communities in which the programs and research are conducted are not spending their own funds in any significant amount on these projects, little oversight has been exercised. The mushroom growth of interest in aging and the aged has paralleled closely the increased availability of Federal dollars from the various agencies. As mentioned previously, the dedication of grant recipients to the aged all too frequently has lasted only as long as have the Federal dollars.

With regard to the dire fiscal status of the Social
Security Trust Fund, this, too, has been a victim of
cavalier mismanagement rather than drained by the aged
pensioners who draw from it. The assumption that a
"trust fund" exists at all is a long standing myth.
Since the government has been quite free to spend trust
fund surpluses, it has done so, leaving only the monies
necessary to pay out the current year's benefits. It is
not the elderly who have decimated the Social Security
Trust Fund; it is the Federal bureaucracy, the Administration and the Congress. According to Dr. W. Allen
Wallis,[4] Chancellor of the University of Rochester and
Chairman in 1974 of the Advisory Committee on Social
Security, the increased Social Security tax rates begun
in 1978 will produce a surplus by 1980 and a projected
growth by 1987 of 140 billion dollars. Although, by law,
the surplus must go to the trust fund, the government can
and will use it, thereby insuring that the trust fund
always will be broke.

The aged beneficiaries of their Federally managed
pension plan have been made the expedient whipping boy
for flagrant government abuse as well as for "a disguised
general tax increase."[5] This concept of the old as a
financial drain is augmented by the almost total emphasis
placed upon the needs and limitations of the elderly in
other aspects of their lives. This reinforces the picture
of older citizens as a burden to be borne by a compassion-
ate younger population. The contrived homogeneity of
the aged based upon their dependency has, in fact, gone
far towards creating an artificial social stratification
system of the old in the United States.

There are indeed Federal programs under which some
of the old are offered employment, provided they are
sufficiently "poor", but such programs require government
organization, regulation and funding. Going a step further, there are volunteer activities for the aged, which
also have required coordinating and, of course, funding
through the auspices of still another Federal agency.
It should be noted that volunteerism under governmental
sponsorship is no longer a simple matter of people help-
ing people through spontaneous coordination of interests
and efforts for a shared purpose. Under the Federal
structure it requires a bureaucracy of many tax paid
employees and a plethora of regulations, requirements,
policies, guidelines and controls. In fact, the purpose
no longer seems to be the spontaniety of individuals
serving other individuals and communities combining
citizen efforts to benefit some aspect of their community

105

life. According to a recent statement by the director
of the Federal volunteer programs, ACTION, "Politics
is a struggle to redistribute power and wealth. That's
what I'm all about."[6] (Emphasis added.) This is an
intriguing revelation of what volunteering has become
under Federal patronage. The questions it raises are:
(1) whether the bureaucracy of ACTION seeks to "redistribute power and wealth," and, if so, to whom and from
whom? and (2) in the ACTION programs for the aged, are
the elderly volunteers informed about the role they are
to play for this ulterior goal?

        Leading the Federal complexity of old age related
activity is the Congress. Not only are there a Senate
Special Committee on Aging and a House of Representatives
Select Committee on Aging, but the Senate Committee also
has seven subcommittees while the House Committee has
four. All are devoted to holding hearings, authorizing
studies and documenting a galaxy of needs, which, subse-
quently, lead to the initiation of more legislation,
more regulated programs, and more spending. In addition,
there is the Subcommittee on Aging of the Senate Committee
on Labor and Public Welfare and there is the Administration's Federal Council on Aging. It has been estimated
that these creative forces had, by 1975, effected some 25
Federal agencies dealing with the aged and at least 50
separate programs, all staffed and funded.[7] And, the
bureaucracy continues to grow.

        As the general public sees the majority of elderly
persons living normal and natural lives, questions even
now are beginning to be asked about mounting costs for
the aged. Not surprisingly, the questions by younger
workers are slanted towards self protection in view of
the hardship of constant inflation, rapidly accelerating
Social Security taxes and the costs of the various programs for older citizens added to all of the other uncontrolled government spending. The old can only suffer
the consequences of their segregated status along with
their victimization by inflation, while the Nation's
policy makers deal with a manageable population adjustment on the basis of political expediency.

                    The Tyranny of Controls

        By definition, a bureaucracy is government adminis-
tration characterized by "a rigid hierarchy of bureaus,
administrators and petty officials" and "excessive red
tape and routine".[8] This definition invites a closer

look at the Federal programs on aging and of the Administration on Aging, official agency in HEW created by Congress in the Older Americans Act.[9] This agency has the power and authority to distribute monies, to institute regulations for their use, and to exercise controls over conformity to these regulations in 50 states and the District of Columbia, in Guam, Puerto Rico, the Virgin Islands and in the Trust Territory of the Pacific Islands. But, this in only the top layer. In each of the ten regional HEW offices, there is a branch of the Administration on Aging staffed to monitor adherence to the Federal regulations by the states in each region. Additionally, AOA has an office in each state or territory charged with implementing the Federal program at the state level, including disbursement of funds, and as another level of oversight for programs and institutions receiving the Federal monies. At the bottom layer are the area agencies distributed throughout the Nation. According to the National Association of Area Agencies on Aging in January, 1979, there were "approximately 570 area agencies on aging" in the fifty-five states and territories, and their distribution ranged from seven states* with only one area agency each to the "50 or more" located in New York state.[10] (The reason for lack of precise information here is not known.) It is at the area agency level that services, mostly for the impoverished elderly, are delivered, but even here the services are usually contracted to other organizations for their delivery. Needless to say, the area agencies also are staffed by directors, coordinators, supervisors and an assortment of other employees. In brief, there is a minimum of three layers of bureaucracy to be crossed usually before any old person reaches one with services. Associated with area agencies, however, it is also possible for individual communities to obtain Federal funds to operate their own aging advocacy and service organization and advisory council, which constitutes a fifth layer in the "strip cake" of bureaucracy. Even at the bottom layers, the Federal office exercises major control over programs to be offered, staffing, and criteria for program operations.

It is easily apparent that, while the old people are citizens of the State, the State and its communities actually have little to do with the programs or with their administration. They are expected only to facilitate the structure and to provide the mandated advisory councils,

*The seven states are Alaska, Delaware, Nevada, New Hampshire, North Dakota, Rhode Island and South Dakota.

committees and required matching monies, the amounts also prescribed by the Federal government.

In addition to the enormous unproductive costs of duplicated and overlapping administration in such a structure, there are other less obvious negative effects. These include: (1) abdication by State administrations of a portion of their responsibility; (2) state legislative compromises and equivocations to obtain Federal dollars; (3) individual political competitiveness to endorse the monied programs and thereby insure a personal place in the sun; and (4) diminution of community official sensitivity to the individuality of its older population. Not the least consequence is the effect upon the elderly themselves, such as, their confusion about which agency gives which service, and their doubts about long held roles and values that appear in conflict with their government's behavior.

With Federally legislated controls dominating the provisions and programs for the aged and for some not so aged, the State House becomes essentially a pass-through agent. By agreeing to conform to the rules, including submission of an annual state plan which has proceeded through all Federal guideline mandated review steps, the Federal money allotment for the state is awarded to the Federally controlled state agency on aging. In so doing, the governor's office, in effect, agrees to ignore the diverse populations of elderly in that state, and they become homogenized into the Nation's aged, all assigned a common character and common needs. Initiative to foster creative, dynamic and innovative ideas to meet different needs and situations tends to melt away. It is enough for a governor to accept an annual report from his advisory board on aging (also required by the Federal government) and to thank them dutifully for their work. Although the state office on aging is a member of the state's official administrative family, its function is quasi-state and Federally controlled.

State legislators, facing frequent elections and living closer to their constituants, are more verbal in their relations with older citizens. This leads to appointment of committees to study elderly needs, permissive legislation for property tax reduction, waiver of college tuition fees, or the lifting of some limited use provisions in statutes to enable localities to deviate from them for the aged. In some instances, legislators appropriate supplementary income benefits for the Federal Supplementary Security Income (SSI) welfare program for elderly recipients. But overall, in the main, legislators raise few questions about the programs in their state and demand no accountability for the Federal programs operating within their districts or for the state as a whole. As politicians, however, some individual legislators adopt a crusading stance on behalf of the aged, lobby for more Federal dollars, become advocates for the old, hold hearings, and publicize the aged "plight". Like their colleagues in the Congress, they have found that a higher percentage of older people vote than do the young. Even when an isolated state legislator asks questions or opposes a bill on the basis of its questionable merit, his voice carries limited weight, since the problems presented are perceived more as Federal matters than as a constituency concern.

At the community level, the government closest to the individual citizens, boards of supervisors and city councils vote their participation in the Federal programs, appoint their representatives to advisory committies, and receive reports. They listen to requests and grant some, especially those that bring Federal dollars for housing and other direct services. They follow regulations. While individual board members attest to their interest in and great concern for the elderly, again no concerted attention is given to changing conditions. No real protest is made against red tape regulations or ineffectual programs. As a result, the city and county bureaucracies also expand in order to maintain and support the problems in accordance with the regulatory controls that undergird the Federal dollars they seek and accept.

Even the critics of public affairs, national news analysts, and the incisive media commentators generally handle Federal programs for the aged with a benign neglect. They appear content to give limited space and time to such subjects as the effects of inflation upon fixed incomes, instances of mistreatment in institutions for the aged, and similar "safe" topics, or others which are essentially superficial. They have not yet cut through the labels and awakened to the realization that a substantial portion of the problems of the aged are the programs for the aged.

When one talks to older persons themselves, their reactions are quietly voiced but are easily identified as perplexity. Even those whose financial status permits them to be the beneficiaries of the government's largess to not understand what is going on. For many others,

their life long values do not permit them to collect
the bounty. For some who do, it is evident that the
price they have paid is too high - too high in embarrassment, in pride and in self respect.

The Price of Paternalism

No doubt the programs initiated for the elderly
poor are viewed by many as beneficent provisions with
noble intent. The major flaw, however, is that these
good intentions enacted into law have characteristics
with the power to hurt. An inherent hazard in paternalism is that it can damage both the receiver and the giver.
To treat adults as children fosters a dependency role that
then gives credence to all the negative attitudes toward
aging. Doling out categorical assistance, such as, a
little money, food or fuel is not unlike a parent's relationship with his child. The difference is that paren-
tal protectiveness of the young is security, but for the
old it is regression with the insecurity of perceived
incapacity and inadequacy.

Admittedly, all old people do not apportion their
resources wisely, but neither do the young. There is
something to be said for the right to be unwise. And,
since most of the aging program administrators are young,
a valid question to be asked is whether they are better
qualified to decide what is best for the elderly than
are the old themselves, long experienced in the art of
living and of surviving.

Paternalism also has unhappy results for the perpe-
trator of this essentially negative relationship. Although a few hundred Congressmen have initiated the condition under law, the total society bears the consequences
of their actions. Once free will in decision making is
compromised for material rewards, the will to be free and
independent also is in jeopardy. This has been demonstrated repeatedly with old people place in institutions,
who, after aggressively fighting for their right to self
determination, finally succumb to the controls and regulations and become passively dependent. It is called
"adjustment" and "cooperation", while, in fact, it is the
tragedy of broken human spirit. The indignity of such
impoverishment of human life is far worse than the impoverishment of simply being economically poor. Further,
when the dependency role of the aged upon government is
accepted, the demands will be unlimited, for the group

so affected will not look within themselves for solutions to any problems. Then, once strong and independent men and women will, in truth, be dependent wards of the state.

This danger now is great. The entire bureaucratic structure staffed by thousands of people has a vested interest in its own perpetuation and, indeed, for further growth of the system. Additionally, politically motivated, self-appointed advocates for the aged demonstrate a psychological need to maintain their superior role of meting out good deeds for "the weak, the lonely and the deprived". They will not easily be appeased with the suggestion that they turn their attention to the few thousands in their own states who truly are frail, sick, lonely and critically in need of all the beneficence that can be mustered for their welfare. In spite of all the obstacles to a policy reversal, however, the American society postpones at its own risk an honest appraisal of the monster it has permitted its representatives to create. The day that the elderly rejoin the mainstream of the Nation's work, wealth, problems and satisfactions, a total citizenry will be richer.

FOOTNOTES

1 Paul Friggens. "Don't Call Me Senior Citizen!" _The Rotarian_. March, 1979. pp. 17-19, 50.

2 Erdman Palmore and Kenneth Morton. "Ageism Compared to Racism and Sexism." _Journal of Gerontology_, Vol. 28, No. 3. 1973. pp. 363-369.

3 Editorial in _Richmond News-Leader_. Richmond, Virginia. February 22, 1978.

4 _Ibid_.

5 _Ibid_.

6 Editorial in _Richmond News-Leader_. Richmond, Virginia. December 3, 1979.

7 "The Elderly in America," _Population Bulletin_, Vol. 30, No. 3. Population Reference Bureau, Inc. Washington, D. C. 1975. p. 20.

8 _The Random House Dictionary of the English Language_. College Edition. 1969.

9 The Older Americans Act of 1965 and subsequent Amendments.

10 Telephone conversation with representative of the National Association of Area Agencies on Aging. Washington, D. C. January 16, 1979.

REFERENCES

Estes, Carroll L. The Aging Enterprise: A Critical Examination of Social Policies and Services for the Aged.
Jossey-Bass, Inc. San Francisco, California. 1979.

Riley, Matilda, et al. Aging and Society, Vol 3: A
Sociology of Age Stratification. Russell Sage
Foundation. New York, New York. 1972.

V

A PHILOSOPHY OF OPTIONS IN A FREE SOCIETY: AN EPILOGUE

Built into the spirit and soul of the United States from the days of its founding has been the freedom of options. Implicit in this freedom are limited government and even less regimentation. The single overriding principle exhorted in the Bill of Rights is non-regimentation, the right to be different. Within the responsible constraints of freedom, this is a guarantee. The entire free enterprise system is premised in equal opportunity to pursue one's destiny, but without any preordained assurance of achievement in success or satisfaction. A nationwide complex of public education affords opportunity for learning, while the option of self-determined benefit remains in place. In short, individual life style or economic role is not regulated, although obstacles to self determined goals may be unequally distributed. To this extent, options have a price in the social order as it has existed.

Resolving a Perplexing Problem

The erosion of commitment to options has been in progress in the United States for several decades. For this reason, it is perhaps not surprising that it would reach a segment of the population as vulnerable as the aged. Once set in motion by awareness of conditions among sick and institutionalized old people, the focus of attention turned then to the elderly population as a whole. Certainly, the fact that they were being retired automatically and pushed out of the mainstream of society in large numbers has had a psychological impact on the general society, producing a rather commonly shared sense of guilt. This, plus admission of the obvious economic effects of uncontrolled inflation, set the stage for consigning to the elderly some of the Federal legislature's inflation spiralling largess. By assigning common characteristics to all older citizens, their universalized problems lent themselves to global solution. Unfortunately, it was at this point that a real problem emerged. With a bit of retrospective wisdom, however, solution is not beyond reach, and the potential damage to old people in the present course will not be realized.

The legislated homogeneity of older citizens is nowhere better demonstrated than in the latest amendments to the Older Americans Act related to social services and effective in 1979. First, Congress has established that an arbitrary fifty per cent of monies allocated for social services must be used only for the elderly who are in "greatest economic and social need". Further, they must be used in very discrete areas to which the Federal government has assigned priority, such as outreach services to obtain other benefits, transportation, telephone reassurance, friendly visitors, home health care, residential renovations, winterization programs, home repair and legal aid. For the most needy older persons, it is difficult to believe that, for the majority, visitors regardless how friendly or attorneys are most critical needs. It is equally inconceivable that the priority needs of all old people will be the same throughout the Nation, identical in Honolulu, Hawaii, and in McMillan, Texas. Since such a program cannot truly serve all the elderly, one can only wonder whether its political value is as great as Congress perceives.

Developed in logical sequence, the Congress and the Federal administration have the authority to undo the capricious statutes and regulations that have evolved as a plethora of bad policies implemented by unnecessary taxes and controls. It will not be easy, for there will be strong opposition from those who have supported and lobbied for the chaos created and from those who derive material gain from it. It may be especially difficult for legislators to admit publicly the errors they enacted into law and for bureaucrats to reduce the reach of their controls. None of these hardships is insurmountable for those who act in good faith.

115

Social Security Trust Fund. A first step is to re-
instate the integrity of the Social Security Trust Fund
and to return the Social Security program to its intended purpose, a Federally administered pension program.
Although this move would be an admission that Social
Security was never intended to be all things to all people, the integrity of the system would be maintained.
The welfare add-ons to the program would be eliminated,
and these provisions then would be treated in a different
fashion, preferably administered at the state level. By
returning the evaluation of needs, people problems and
their solutions to the states in which they are endemic,
a step would be taken towards insuring that each governmental jurisdiction knows its own citizens. This would
encourage the resumption in each state of responsibility
to and for its citizens on a more personal level. The
fact that welfare programs might be different from one
state to another could be healthy with a potential for
constructive, innovative change.

A final step in restoring Social Security would be
for the Federal government to make good on its I.O.U.'s
to the Trust Fund. To ask the honest repayment of the
total debt would be expecting the unattainable, since
this was never the intent. Nevertheless, since these
monies were "borrowed" for General Fund purposes, the
General Fund should repay some percentage of them. A
statute then is in order to protect the Trust Fund for its
beneficiaries and against all future marauding custodians
of the National interests. At this point, the Social
Security tax could be substantially reduced and still insure that the Trust Fund would be more than adequate to
meet both current and future needs. Perhaps the most
positive gain from this newly instituted integrity of the
pension fund would be psychological. An earned pension
could not then be confused with charity. At the present,
this differentiation is no longer clear.

Welfare Provisions for the Aged. The present Supplementary Security Income Program (SSI) administered by
Social Security is the welfare program that replaced
Federal grants to the states for the aged, blind and disabled. In June, 1978, the maximum SSI payment to couples
went to $284.10 a month and for individuals to $189.40 a
month.[1] These are maximum payments when all qualifying
requirements are met. With annual incomes of $3,409.20
(couple) and $2,272.80 (single), the program does not in-
sure an adequate standard of living. Since SSI payments
do not produce minimally adequate subsistance levels for
those who qualify for them, it is necessary that recipi-

116

ents abase themselves further by applying for good stamps, surplus food, subsidized housing, Medicaid and all the rest. Surely there is a better way!

For a beginning, those who are unfortunate enough in old age to need public assistnace should receive it with dignity and respect, regardless of the reasons for their present need. Far better would be a minimum living income paid in a single check to be disbursed by the recipient according to his individual priorities of needs and values. If he could supplement this with a small job or other activity, his public income would not be affected. Certainly, all would not spend their money wisely, but this is an option no less treasured by the old than by the young.

In order to assure that the States and their local jurisdictions carry out their responsibility to their own citizens, each state should administer this aspect of its welfare program as one component of the total program, determining a reasonable living income on the basis of its own economy. Insofar as the elderly over age 65 are concerned, however, the only national provision that appears to be in order is that none would be below an established base minimum, perhaps utilizing a formula that defines minimum in relation to median income in each state. This woudl replace the demeaning Federal "handout" programs with their confusing regulations and multiple means tests. For the minority of those receiving public income or income supplement in order to achieve the accepted minimum, and whose health or circumstances demanded extra expendiures, a program under local supervision would be aware of this need and have the opportunity to draw upon contingency plans to meet it.

By abandoning the proliferation of programs and funds now in use for the aged, including the bureaucracy that runs them, monies would be available for this approach. Additionally, if that portion of current Federal taxes were left in the State, the high cost of their trip to Washington would also remain in the State, thereby enhancing their purchasing value for useful purposes. Smaller Federal taxes and somewhat higher State taxes would produce sufficient revenue to support State jurisdictional programs, while the total cost to the taxpayer would be lowered.

Although not writing about the elderly but about the total gamut of national welfare programs in the United States, syndicated columnist Michael Novak [2] (January 13,

1979) reported rather startling facts about the cost of present fragmented welfare programs and their top-heavy administration. The conclusion he reached, based upon census data and annual welfare costs, was that direct income payments to welfare recipients without the exhorbitant bureaucratic costs would provide generous family incomes far in excess of any now paid. More specifically, he pointed out that total yearly expenditures for social welfare programs increased from $50 billion in 1960 to $171 billion in 1971. This $121 billion increase alone would have provided for each of the 25 million poor persons, reported by the U. S. Census Cureau, an annual stipend of $4800, or for a family of four an income of $19,200. If this is true for the general welfare population, it would be no less true for the elderly who are in this poverty category. Support for Mr. Novak's view can be found in a report from the Institute for Research on Poverty, University of Wisconsin.[3]

A far more simple solution to welfare needs of the elderly could be achieved in the states by a routine procedure based upon minimum acceptable income balanced against retirement income. When one reaches age 65, or when he or she files for retirement after age 65, a single form would be filed in a designated office of the State charged with administration of supplemental income. This form would show verified amounts of Social Security, other annual persions, annuity income, wages for full-time or part-time work, income from savings and investments, or related sources, for self and spouse. Should the retirement income total fall below the established minimum essential income in his state of residence, the difference would be paid to the retiree by the State. Since filing this information would be optional, should financial circumstances deteriorate or living cost demands escalate as the result of disability, it could be filed in later years. None of this need be complicated to the point of harrassment. Each year a mail-in updated verification of income could be required.

In order to cushion further the impact of reduced retirement income and to encourage individual financial preparation for future retirement, a major incentive would be to eliminate the Federal and State taxes on interest derived from savings accounts. The precedent for this incentive to save is world-wide, a common tax concession in many nations. This change would remove the disincentive to save, especially for lower and moderate income persons who are far more apt to have savings

118

accounts than investments in stocks and bonds. Eliminating this taxation should have the effect of encouraging saving, a practice that seems to be eroding in the United States. With greater motivation from the tangible benefits of saving, self-reliance and self-responsibility might well become more widespread in the future.

"Senior Citizen" Programs. Among all of the older American programs, probably the most prevalent are the Title VII Nutrition Programs and Senior Centers (included under Title III beginning in 1979). Both of these have a strong "socializing" component. The Nutrition Program serves a relatively small percentage of older persons, even when every effort is made to solicit their attendance, including providing transportation and sending out canvasers to lure elderly people to the sites. Like the Nutrition Program, Senior Centers contribute to segregation of the elderly. Far better are the old community centers with activities that appeal to all age groups, some separate and others together where interests cross age lines. Here the old are a part of the community, not apart from it.

Since there is a strong emphasis in both the Nutrition Program and the Senior Center Program upon recreation and leisure activities, they also tend to emphasize the old population as one to be amused. In large measure, however, this is a work oriented group, who enjoy leisure and recreation as a part of life, not as the whole of it. Furthermore, when one works at recreation, it ceases to be a leisure pursuit and, in fact, becomes work. Because most people now grown old are mature individuals, they do not need or want constant companionship either with those their own age or younger. They have inner resources that allow them to spend some of their time in pursuit of quiet activities during which aloneness is not lonely. Finally, there is a strong possibility that many of the "aged programs" contribute to the isolation of older people, shunting them further into and old age social stratification and lessening their opportunities to be an integral part of the work and play of the total population.[5]

Judging solely from what the elderly themselves say, they prefer to live their lives as they wish and much as they have lived earlier. They want to be useful, and the greater number are seldom lonely. The vast majority live near some of their family, and see them frequently. Competent and accessible health care and an adequate income to meet spiraling costs are their major concerns. There is little indication that they need or want to be

119

"programmed", although they like open doors to those
things in which they are interested. Some like clubs
and much social participation; others do not. Some enjoy a great deal of physical activity; others like to
sit and watch the action. In brief, they are as different one from the other as they have always been, perhaps
even more so in old age. None of this suggests that any
National program for the aged can be sufficiently wise
to meet a common need, to have a common appeal, or to
offer the options the aged want and deserve.

Self Determination

The whole idea of options is one of choice and self
determination. Implicit in this are not only the rights
and privileges of independence, but also the obligations
and duties. It is in the meshing of the composite ingredients of responsible citizenship that a man or woman
actually exercises self determination. Those now old have
lived intimately with this conceptual structure as the
foundation of their value standards. They are well aware
of the constraints of freedom, but, within the limits,
they associate their dignity, integrity and self worth
with the right and responsibility of making their own
decisions about their own lives. When this freedom is
taken away or threatened, their equal citizenship is compromised.

For persons now old, their perception of the role of
government is in the tradition of "government of, by and
for the people", not of citizens as puppets of the State.
For this reason, they do not understand the obstacles and
restrictions that government now imposes upon their lives.

Admittedly, there are those in the old age category
who do accept and even welcome government benefactions,
and who apparently accept the conditions for receiving
them. In every age group, there is a segment of people
who are essentially dependent, some by their nature and
personality, and others who have been bred in dependency
by a lifelong reliance upon public cofers and services
for subsistence. Certainly in old age, they cannot be
expected to change. But among the old, those who want
charity are a distinct minority. Public policy regard-
ing old citizens in retirement needs to be constructed
for a broadly based population, including, (1) the majority who need only alternative options as time and circumstances produce change, (2) the self-providers whose

120

resources become inadequate, and (3) the ones who have required public support throughout life. It should be conceded, however, that the old are the least appropriate segment of the population on whom to impose sweeping social change or to subject to intrusive forces. Monies paid to the young to regulate and manage the lives of the aged could be used far more productively in facilitating lifestyles already established.

In one state with approximately 600,000 citizens eligible for Older Americans Act programs (age 60 and above), the State Agency reports that approximately one-third of the eligible use the programs. This State receives some $13,000,000 from the Federal government for disbursement. Since it is reported that $5 million of this total amount is spent in the Nutrition Program (which appears to serve fewer than 9,000 full-time equivalents in a year), this means that very little benefit is derived for the remaining approximately 191,000 of the composite service reach after administrative and operational costs are deducted. A case in point is one community in which the area agency had a 1978 total social service budget of a little over $66,000. Approximately $16,000 of this was spent in social services to elderly persons, while the remainder, or nearly $50,000, over 75 per cent of that budget, was for administration and operations. Another instance is an area agency with a social service budget of nearly $150,000 of which approximately 85 per cent was consumed by administration and operations. Who are the major beneficiaries? Obviously, they are the not-so-elderly program employees who direct, manage and control the program.

Essentially ignored by the government up to this point are areas of valid concern to the elderly and for which no lavish monetary expenditures by government would be needed, especially if all older persons had a living income and available assured protections. Paramount among these needs is competent health maintenance, but there are almost no trained geriatric specialists in the country. Medical schools could prepare physicians-in-training with basic skills to understand and treat old patients. Failure to do so has not been lack of money, but lack of interest. The same is true in other aspects of health services. This condition prevails despite the knowledge that prevention of serious illness and treatment for chronic health problems are an important key to a life of independence.

121

Another need area to which private sector attention can be invited is that of housing options for different life styles. All old people do not accept the popular alternative of government controlled high rise apartments that meet security requirements as the only alternative to their own houses. Almost every housing preference found among young persons has its counterpart among the elderly, except perhaps the size. Where options are available, they are exercised, and often there are waiting lists. Creative and innovative use of existing buildings has considerable potential as does the specially designed small house neighborhood within the larger community. Numerous possibilities exist in a wide range of prices and social environments, although they have received scant attention and even less implementation. With an adequate income and given housing choices, the old will find the housing suited to their needs, income and preferences.

Frail and Sick Elderly. One segment of the older population that draws considerable attention and is a basis for justification of program expansion and increasing government controls is the frail and sick elderly. These comprise perhaps 20 per cent of the total older population. Approximately 15 per cent of the aged live in communities but are restricted in strength and function and need assistance in activities of daily living; and another 5 per cent are in nursing homes or other custodial care institutions. This population includes those who manage with the support and assistance of their families, as well as others who have outlived their families or whose families are unable or unwilling to meet their needs.

For the estimated one million in nursing homes and other facilities, there are more than adequate laws to cover both their care and treatment. The surveillance of the facilities to insure compliance must rest with the individual states and territories and with local authorities. To be sure, the job is not done adequately, but the solution lies with the public-at-large and its authorized representatives, not with bureaucrats in the Nation's Capital. Enforcement of standards of quality of care will be as rigid as the citizens of a state demand and the best ombudsman will be an alert and informed citizenry.

Excluding the institutionalized elderly, this leaves approximately 3 to 3.4 million who belong in the category of frail and sick in the communities of the states and territories, or an average of 60,000 in each of these jurisdictions. Obviously, these will not be distributed equally among the states. Regardless of this unequal distribution, the problem is one of manageable proportions. Since many of these individuals are in family settings and have needed supports, the minority dependent upon public aid and protection is a still smaller number.

For those in families and who lack private income, the state welfare provisions proposed would allow these elderly to meet many personal needs as well as lessen the financial strain on the families when their incomes are inadequate for the additional necessary costs. In the instances where there is no family available to care, and where the aged individual cannot safely live without the numerous supports of food preparation, shopping, medical surveillance, home maintenance and the other essentials to independence, assured income could purchase feasible alternatives. Some of the congregate living alternatives can offer considerable variety in extent of privacy, life style choice, and freedom to exercise the highest level of independence possible, while, at the same time, affording nourishing meals, housekeeping assistance, medication monitoring and other assurances of needed support on a continuous basis. The continuity of this security could actually lessen stress and facilitate a longer life of greater independence. In contrast, the proliferation of fragmented services offered to a relative few under a variety of programs can constitute an added burden of needed adjustments without any confidence that help will be available when needed. Additionally, the cost of such services is exorbitant.

Since the problems for the frail elderly and those with restricting serious chronic conditions can generally be expected to occur more frequently in very old age, many of the aged population can expect to live out their entire lives without becoming totally dependent upon others. This is demonstrated repeatedly by financially secure older people in supportive communities for the elderly and even in apartment complexes, good quality residential hotels, and other housing adapted for this purpose. Here canes, walkers and wheel chairs facilitate movement rather than deny it. A good place to start in dealing with this problem could be for the Federal government to turn over all control of "Senior Housing" to the states in which it is located. These buildings then could be modified, staffed and rededicated to this area

123

of unmet housing need for the frail elderly.

Within each state and the communities of the state, desires and needs of the various segments of the population can and should be known. It is within these jurisdictions that appropriate and feasible plans to meet citizen needs, including elderly citizens, can be made effectively and with relevant participation by those affected. Perhaps the assumption of such responsibility at state and local levels is not an option, since, in fact, to do less is an abdication of the responsibility freely accepted by elected officials.

The whole concept of State responsibility and the ultimate suitability of State relationship to its citizens is reinforced by a question recently posed by the U. S. Commissioner on Aging[7] when he asked, "How can be halt the fragmentation, waste the duplication that have come with the proliferation of programs for the elderly?" His response to that very valid question, however, seems to be a key to the problem - not a solution.

> State and local governments, without adequate resources and lacking necessary authority, have not been able to manage their basic responsibilities to the elderly. And they show no inclination to face up to the serious problems older people confront, without significant Federal initiative. The quest for comprehensive community services must begin in Washington. (Emphasis added.)

Since when did the States not have all the authority needed to exercise basic responsibilities to their citizens? The people of the State are the authority. Is it not possible that the "adequate resources" are going to Washington, and, were they retained in the States, would be adequate? Is it possible there is not a capability in the States for managing their peoples' affairs without "Federal initiative"? Must services in the community begin in Washington? Surely, the arrogance of this statement is the root of the problem. In truth, the admitted "fragmentation, waste and duplication" and the "proliferation of programs" are the product of the Federal assumption of control for which the elderly now pay the consequences.

The aged are not a problem, although some of them have problems as do persons of all ages. In retrospect and after reviewing the various "aging" programs and

124

their consequences, it appears that a major problem for the old is the plethora of Federal aging programs. With the exception of Social Security and Medicare, were the others to be terminated, the most traumatic effects would be upon the vast bureaucracy that controls them and the professionals who feed upon them. Despite the high costs, the reach of the Federal programs is limited and the "benefits" more symbolic than real.

FOOTNOTES

1

"Memorandum." Special Committee on Aging, United States Senate. Senator Frank Church, Chairman. Washington, D. C. June 19, 1978.

2

Michael Novak. "'Lord Protectors of the Poor' Claim Superiority." Syndicated Column. Richmond News-Leader. Richmond, Virginia. January 13, 1979.

3

"Progress Against Poverty: 1964-1974." Focus on Poverty Research, Vol. I, No. 1, Spring-Summer, 1976. Institute for Research on Poverty. University of Wisconsin. Madison, Wisconsin. pp. 8-12.

4

Carroll R. Melton. "Housing Finance and Homeownership: Public Policy Initiatives in Selected Countries." International Union of Building Societies and Savings Associations. Chicago, Illinois. 1978. pp. 10-14.

5

Arnold M. Rose. Older People and Their Social World. F. A. Davis Company. Philadelphia, Pennsylvania. 1965. pp. 3-16.

6

Betty Booker. "Act Imperils Non-Priority Aid to Aged." Richmond Times Dispatch. Richmond, Virginia. January 14, 1979, and personal communication.

7

Robert Benedict. "Aging Policy - What's Needed." Modern Maturity, Vol. 21, No. 4. American Association of Retired Persons. Washington, D. C. 1978. p. 10.